Roderick Nash was born in New York City and studied
history at Harvard University and at the University of
Wisconsin with Merle Curti. Now Professor of History
and Environmental Studies at the University of California,
Santa Barbara, he is best known for his book *Wilderness
and the American Mind*. His other writings include *The
Rights of Nature: A History of Environmental Ethics*;
From These Beginnings; and *American Environmentalism*.

The Nervous Generation: American Thought, 1917-1930

Roderick Nash
With a New Preface by the Author

Elephant Paperbacks
Ivan R. Dee, Publisher, Chicago

THE NERVOUS GENERATION. Copyright © 1970 by Rand McNally and Co. This book was originally published in 1970 and is here reprinted by arrangement with the author.

First ELEPHANT PAPERBACK edition published 1990 by Ivan R. Dee, Inc., 1332 North Halsted Street, Chicago 60622. Manufactured in the United States of America.

Library of Congress Cataloging-in-Publication Data
    The nervous generation: American thought, 1917–1930 / Roderick Nash; with a new preface by the author.
    Reprint. Originally published: Chicago: Rand McNally, 1970. Includes bibliographical references.
    ISBN 0-929587-21-9
    1. United States—Intellectual life—20th century. 2. United States—Civilization—1918–1945. I. Title.
    E169.1.N367   1990
    973.91—dc20   89-38691

Preface to the 1990 Edition

". . . the hell with her lost-generation talk and all the dirty,
easy labels . . . [it's] a lot of rot. . . ."
                                        —Ernest Hemingway (c. 1921)

The 1920s is a strong candidate for the most thoroughly documented non-war decade in American history—with biographies and autobiographies, historical syntheses and monographic studies, novels, books of photographs, television series and motion pictures. But despite (or, more accurately, *because of*) this attention, serious misconceptions about the decade persist. It was in the hope of questioning the lost generation–roaring twenties–jazz age stereotype that I wrote *The Nervous Generation* in 1970. Critics have been sufficiently generous to call the book a major reinterpretation. I would be satisfied, however, if it has helped students of history better understand the relationship between continuity and change over time.

The first dragon to slay is the demon of the *decade*. This is not an easy task. The years that end with "0" exert a compelling force on historical understanding. We speak and write glibly about the 1920s and the 1950s or the 1960s as if they stand apart as islands in the flow of time, connected, presumably, by the tenuous bridges of New Year's Eve. So we are led to believe there is "fifties music," "sixties hairstyles" and "twenties thought."

Granted there are sounds and appearances and ideas that can be linked with a ten-year span. But they did not begin on the first day of a decade and end on the last. Moreover, they were certainly not the only forms present in the years in question. Crewcuts could be found in the 1960s, and rock 'n' roll music did not throw sentimental ballads off the charts in the preceding decade. Revolutions and watersheds (more accurately, if you care about geography, water *divides*) are primitive tools in the study of history of thought and culture. In *A Moveable Feast* Hemingway was right in calling them "dirty, easy labels" (see the headquote above), although a few years later he changed his mind and adopted the "lost generation" characterization with a vengeance. What makes historical labeling and periodization by decades so difficult to avoid is that it is much easier to paste names on the past than to disentangle its complexities and ambivalences.

Another foe of truth in history is the power of the bizarre. Historians, like journalists and conversationalists, are suckers for the dramatic. The new and unusual are much more likely to receive attention than the commonplace and everyday. This tendency makes for good entertainment but at the price of historical accuracy. Particularly when the task at hand is understanding an entire society over a span of years, there are serious pitfalls in overgeneralizing from a few eye-catching pieces of evidence to the character of the age.

The 1920s, like all decades, were a blending of old and new. Despite the many labels, the changes that occurred in these years were not sudden and revolutionary but glacial. When an unprecedented idea or mode of behavior appeared, it did not destroy older forms. Rather, new and old existed alongside each other in a condition historians of thought call ambivalence. To say, then, that ideas change is really only to say that the proportion of new to old shifts—one loses a little ground while the other makes a small gain. Consequently the spirit or mood of a decade, or of any era, is not monolithic but a many-faceted complex of often contradictory ideas and actions.

When I set out to write about the 1920s I was confronted with one of the most powerful stereotypes in American historiography: the myth of the lost generation, the roaring twenties, the jazz age. Since I hoped to write a fresh analysis, I decided to take nothing for granted. First of all I asked whether everyone alive in the United States between 1920 and 1930 fitted this image. The answer was almost self-evident: many, probably the great majority, did not feel lost at all. Like a powerful dye in a tub of water, the glamorous escapades and daring ideas of a few had colored historical understanding of the multitude.

Second, I questioned how lost was lost. Having spent considerable parts of my life in wildernesses, I took a literal approach to the definition. To be lost is to be bewildered, confused, and insecure; it does not make for happy camping. One's overwhelming urge is to get found or to find oneself. Indeed, there is a lot of *nervousness* about being lost. The members of a nervous generation, I concluded, could be expected either to hold more tightly to what was old and familiar or to make every effort to find new meanings with which to order their lives. Neither of these responses squared with the cynical, debauched, nihilistic reputation of the 1920s. Phrased another way, I did not question that some of the old gods and guidelines were losing relevance after 1920. Instead I wondered if the analysis generally made of this phenomenon went far enough.

Over the last twenty years what a number of students and professional historians have found most interesting about *The Nervous Generation* is its use of evidence from popular culture. My discussion of headline-making crimes, sports heroes, best-selling books, censorship and morality, "pop" religion, and the eccentricities of Henry Ford has been well received, I think, because it reflected and influenced changes in the nature of historical documentation and in the scope of history itself. In the past twenty years or so, scholars interested in "popular cultural history" and the "new social history" have paid increasing attention to the informal side of American civilization. There is new interest in what went on behind the scenes of national politics and economics.

What captured the enthusiasm of ordinary people? How can we explain popularity and the changing taste in heroes? The answers to these questions, I believe, tell more about the climate of opinion in any era than does standard political history. The most genuine insights into the ideas and values of people come not from watching them work but from watching them play.

So, much of what you will read in the following pages will not be familiar from textbooks and formal history. But you may find reasons for reexamining the generalizations which the historical profession has advanced without much opposition for more than half a century.

R N.

Santa Barbara, California
October 1989

Contents

The Nervous Generation

Chapter 1

Introduction

Next to names like F. Scott Fitzgerald, Ernest Hemingway, and Henry L. Mencken, those of Gene Stratton-Porter, Zane Grey, and Harold Bell Wright have stirred little interest among historians of American thought and culture in the period between World War I and the Depression. Yet during these years books by the latter three appeared sixteen times on the national lists of best-sellers, while the works of the first three never appeared at all. Grey's westerns were among the top ten works of fiction every year from 1917 to 1924. Twice they were number one; twice number three. But even Grey may have been outsold in the postwar decade by an author who was not even taken seriously by the custodians of the rankings—Edgar Rice Burroughs, of the Tarzan sagas. Fitzgerald, by contrast, never ranked among the best-selling American authors of the 1920s; *This Side of Paradise* (1920) only found some fifty thousand buyers in the first few years after its publication, while the sale of Wright's *The Re-Creation of Brian Kent* (1920) approached a million copies. Mencken's appeal was highly esoteric while Hemingway's name did not make the top ten until 1940. Grey, Stratton-Porter, Wright, and Burroughs, moreover, conveyed an old-fashioned message quite at odds with that of the big names.

1

These discoveries prompted a series of questions about American thought in the 1920s that led to the book at hand.

With few exceptions the general public and scholars alike have been captured and captivated by the "lost generation–roaring twenties" image of the twenties. American intellectuals supposedly emerged from the war years cynical and alienated. Rebellion became a way of life: they drifted, valueless, from bar to bar and bedroom to bedroom, members of the lost generation. Popular thought in the 1920s has also been subject to extensive mythologizing. We have been led to believe that this was the "jazz age," as F. Scott Fitzgerald labeled it in 1922, during which Americans either indulged in an orgy of irresponsible dissipation or pursued the main chance with a narrow concentration that permitted neither ethics nor altruism. It was a decade-long house party. Iconoclasm was the order of the day. Tradition and convention were so much cumbersome rubbish. The war had exposed the hollowness of the past, and the twenties turned against it savagely. So the portrait is usually painted.

While too much has been made of World War I as an influence on American thought, the spectacle of war and the frustrations of the peace did leave many citizens bewildered and shaken. But the logic that proceeds from this point to brand the twenties as a time of cynicism and rebellion, verging on nihilism, is questionable. Bewilderment and insecurity are not acceptable conditions for most persons. When one is lost, he seeks, desperately, to be found—or to find himself. The same might be said of a society. The decade after the war was a time of heightened anxiety when intellectual guideposts were sorely needed and diligently sought. Many clung tightly to the familiar moorings of traditional custom and value. Others actively sought new ways of understanding and ordering their existence. Americans from 1917 to 1930 constituted a *nervous* generation, groping for what certainty they could find. The conception of this time as one of resigned cynicism and happy reveling leaves too much American thought and action unexplained to be satisfactory.

An incomplete understanding of a small group of literati has shaped the understanding of American intellectual history in the 1920s. Intellectuals were by no means unanimous in professing the disillusionment of the expatriates, bohemians, and satirists, and even the degree to which *they* expressed it is moot. For a great many thoughtful Americans World War I did not mean intellectual derailment. The threads of continuity in the history of ideas are visible across the war years, as they are across most so-called watersheds. Henry May's *The End of American Innocence* (1959) and Morton White's conception of a "revolt against formalism" notwithstanding, prewar ideas and ideals continued into the twenties with scarcely a hitch. Indeed the war and the resulting nervousness prompted large numbers of Americans to give even stronger affirmation to values that had allegedly ended by 1920.

Some intellectuals, to be sure, redefined the nature of value. The change, however, has been represented as greater than it actually was. While criticizing the method of the absolutists and the genteel tradition, the relativists preserved much of the content of the older creed.

At the fringe of the American intellectual community stood a few really shaken minds for whom neither the old absolutism nor the new relativism and scientism sufficed as a basis for belief. Yet even these disillusioned few refused to exist with no values at all. Instead they began the American exploration of a point of view later labeled *existentialism*. Axiomatic to this position was confrontation with human futility and the absurdity of life. For this reason these intellectuals' conception of themselves as a lost generation was essential. Such a pose was part of a deliberate artistic experiment, an attempt not to deny value but rather to create from their own frustrated lives existential situations in which radically new values could be formulated. Despair and disillusion were dramatized in order to accentuate the achievement of confronting reality. Ernest Hemingway, F. Scott Fitzgerald, Joseph Wood Krutch, and the malcontented minority they represented were lost only by traditional standards. In their own terms they were finding new ways of defining and keeping a new faith.

As for popular thought in the 1920s, there has likewise been overemphasis on the revolutionary and bizarre. We have read (and with the aid of records, television, and motion pictures, heard and seen) so much about the flapper, the bootlegger, and the jazz band that our conception of the era is greatly distorted. The 1920s were more than these things, just as the 1960s have been more than the jet set, hippies, and *Playboy*. We have forgotten F. Scott Fitzgerald's 1931 admonition that the jazz age concept he coined applied only to the "upper tenth of [the] nation." Perhaps even this was generous.

The point is that evidence for generalizing about the mood of the decade is frequently incomplete, often by design. The twenties has been given little chance except to roar.

In fact, popular thought in these years was remarkably conservative. Beneath the eye-catching outward iconoclasm, the symbolic revolt, was a thick layer of respect for time-honored American ways, means, and rationales. The same nervousness that induced intellectuals to search for certainty prompted the general public to cling to familiar ideas with nearly hysterical intensity. It is difficult to square the popular taste of the 1920s in heroes, literature, religion, and politics, for instance, with the stereotype of the jazz age.

Chapter 2

Reputation

Popularizers

History, Voltaire believed, is only a pack of tricks we play on the dead. Thinking so, he would have chortled over the historiography of American thought in the 1920s, because the decade has proven a particularly fertile field for mythmakers. Fresh interpretation demands that one first come to terms with the reputation of these years. Yet the depth to which the stereotype of the twenties has been stamped into our consciousness makes this a difficult task. Particularly for those who were adults in the 1930s (and most of the people to whom we owe our present knowledge of the 1920s were), the postwar decade is invariably seen through the screen of the Crash and Depression. As a result the twenties have been represented either as a golden, carefree time of happy irresponsibility or as a blind, cynical time of disastrous irresponsibility.

No one has done more to shape the conception of the American 1920s than Frederick Lewis Allen. His *Only Yesterday: An Informal History of the 1920s,* published in 1931, has been the font at which most subsequent writers about the decade initially drank. Allen was a Bostonian by birth, educated at Groton and Harvard, and precisely thirty years old in 1920. Three years later he began a connection with *Harper's Magazine* that carried him to its editorship in 1941, a post he held until 1953, the year before his death. Allen did not regard himself as a professional historian. His forte was journalism, reporting and commenting on matters that appeared in the press "only yesterday." Yet Allen deserves more attention than he has hitherto received as a pioneer in American social and intellectual history. In *Only Yesterday* he has declared it his purpose to delineate "the changing state of the public mind ... the fashions, ideas, and general atmosphere of the period." Given the few precedents for this kind of history, Allen did remarkably well. His account, moreover, enjoyed immediate popularity. The year following its publication, 1932, *Only Yesterday* appeared in second place on the list of best-selling nonfiction. Aided by its selection as a Book-of-the-Month Club offering and the basis of a motion picture, it sold over half a million copies to 1952, and a 1964 paperback edition is currently extending this record.

Allen's interpretation of American intellectual history in the 1920s is based on the idea of an interregnum. He has called the years between the Armistice and the Crash a "new era," "a time of revolution," a period when "everything seemed meaningless and unimportant" because new values had not yet been created out of the shambles left by the war. *Only Yesterday* has been the first to give wide publicity to the idea that Americans suffered a comprehensive, decade-long letdown after World War I. The bubble of idealism that had buoyed the nation during the fighting burst suddenly when peace came. The American people were left "restless," "discontented," "disillusioned," "spiritually tired." It appeared that "life was futile and nothing mattered much." According to Allen, this perspective proved conducive to an "eat, drink, and be merry for tomorrow we die" mentality.

Young Americans of both sexes, *Only Yesterday* argues, responded immediately and completely, embarking on a full-fledged "revolution in manners and morals." But "men and women of every age in every part of the country" did not lag far behind in experimenting with the new standards of deportment and attitude. The result, Allen would have us believe, was the roaring twenties, "the ballyhoo years." With compelling skill he has sketched in the details: the speculative mania, the fads and crazes, the vogue of the lurid and lewd in press and motion picture. The dominant impression *Only*

Yesterday creates is of a world of hip flasks, rumbleseats, raccoon coats, crossword puzzles, marathon dances, and ticker tape through which whirled a slightly demented citizenry.

Although dominated in large part by the blare and glare, *Only Yesterday* does recognize that beneath the ballyhoo was a layer of insecurity and unhappiness. Allen has occasionally noted that many Americans did crave "a new set of enduring satisfactions." Sometimes they weren't even so new. While discussing the excitement of Charles A. Lindbergh's 1927 flight across the Atlantic Ocean, Allen has suggested that the public was eager for an old-style hero. Lindbergh's feat appealed to a nation that was "spiritually starved." Allen sees the idolization of Lindbergh as "a vast religious revival," a celebration of the wholesomeness, dedication, courage, and romance that had been part of the old order and was still needed in the 1920s.

Allen has begun his chapter on intellectuals in the twenties with a quotation from F. Scott Fitzgerald that was destined to become standard equipment in most subsequent discussions of this topic. It appears in the final paragraphs of Fitzgerald's *This Side of Paradise* (1920): "here was a new generation . . . grown up to find all Gods dead, all wars fought, all faiths in man shaken." Allen has not used the other omnipresent quotation, attributed to Gertrude Stein, about a "lost generation," but his analysis supports this stereotype. Intellectuals in the twenties, Allen has written, found that "certainty had departed life . . . nothing . . . was sure . . . there was no solid thing on which a man could lay hold and say, This is real; this will abide." Fixed values had collapsed, and the highbrows were in revolt against the mainstream of American civilization. All they possessed, Allen contends, was a vague credo deifying individual freedom and deploring repression and conformity.

In the concluding pages of *Only Yesterday*, Allen has stated that the collapse of the stock market occasioned a change in the American mood. The revolt of the highbrows, the ballyhoo, the breathless excitement at smashing taboos, the cynicism and the speculation gave way, and with them what Allen has styled the temper of the twenties. By the 1930s "the mood of intellectual disillusionment was passing; the garment of hopeless resignation began to look a little worn at the elbows." For Allen himself even 1931 was a suitable vantage point for smiling at the memory of "those charming, crazy days" and forgetting the "aching disillusionment" and the "spiritual paralysis." The 1920s, for him, were already becoming "the good old days."

Only Yesterday has left its many readers with the impression that the end of World War I marked the start of a radically new era in the history of American thought. Seizing on the decade's most glamorous aspects and generalizing from a few headlines to "the American people," Allen has succeeded in creating the belief that everyone in the twenties was either a rebellious hedonist, a rootless cynic, or a materialistic monomaniac. The book's most durable bequest to later interpreters has been the idea that older American values, traditions, and ideals meant little or nothing to the 1920s.

After his initial success with *Only Yesterday*, Frederick Lewis Allen turned to the 1930s, publishing *Since Yesterday* in 1940. Once again there is the sense of the twenties as an interregnum. In the preface Allen has made the point that, whereas the thirties were preoccupied with serious economic and political matters, in the twenties "trivialities... had been the essence of life in the United States." *I Remember Distinctly: A Family Album of the American People, 1918–1941* (1947) illustrates this point vividly. It is an oversize book of photographs and other illustrative material assembled by Allen's wife, Agnes Rogers, with running comment by her husband. But the pictures tell the story. Here are the "fabulous nineteen-twenties," complete with flagpole sitters, marathon dancers, movie stars, gangsters, sports heroes, and California "personality girls."

In 1952 Allen published his final word on the 1920s in *The Big Change: America Transforms Itself, 1900–1950*, which was also a Book-of-the-Month Club selection. Twenty years had not changed his mind. The twenties were still a time of "tremendous trivia" in which "disillusionment and rebellion" gripped Americans. The effect of this volume, as of Allen's previous work, has been to focus attention on the sensational. The gap that normally separates history from journalism has been virtually erased, and the result is distortion.

Second only to Frederick Lewis Allen as a major architect of the reputation of the 1920s is another Harvard man and long-time Washington corespondent, Mark Sullivan. The book that made him famous was a six-volume "contemporary history" entitled *Our Times: The United States, 1900–1925*. The first volume, covering the Theodore Roosevelt years, appeared in 1926 and captured public favor to the extent of placing fourth on the best-seller non-fiction lists. Sullivan published Volume VI, *The Twenties*, nine years later. Undoubtedly Allen's 1931 study had stolen some of his thunder, but Sullivan's book was widely read. More important for purposes of the general reputation of the twenties, it has filtered into the public consciousness in such a way that it has shaped the thinking of people who, as likely as not, had never heard of Mark Sullivan.

Much of *Our Times*, Volume VI, is political history "disinfected," Sullivan believes, of "romantic legend." Not until Chapter 16 does the account turn to intellectual history. Sullivan begins with a portrait of the "stony disillusionment" with which he feels the American people reacted to World War I. Taking Ernest Hemingway as a case study, he quotes a passage from *A Farewell to Arms* (1929) that has been reiterated time and again as later historians have attempted to articulate their conception of the spirit of the postwar decade: "I was always embarrassed by the words 'sacred,' 'glorious,' and 'sacrifice,' and the expression 'in vain.' We had heard them ... and read them, on proclamations ... for a long time, and I had seen nothing sacred, and the things that were glorious had no glory and the sacrifices were like the stockyards at Chicago if nothing was done with the meat except to bury it." Trite now, this was the first time that the quotation was employed in an historical work. It makes its point well so far as Hemingway and a few other Americans actually involved in the war were concerned, but Sullivan is guilty of overstatement in claiming that "Hemingway spoke for an era."

This same tendency to generalize from an individual in special circumstances to the entire nation is apparent in Sullivan's section entitled "The 'Lost Generation.'" Allen used the phrase without quotation marks, without emphasis, and without reference to Hemingway or Gertrude Stein. But Sullivan has publicized it in connection with these literati and in particular with Hemingway's *The Sun Also Rises* (1926), and in so doing he has again begun a tradition that most subsequent commentators on the intellectuals of the twenties were to follow. To his credit, however, Sullivan seems to be somewhat uncertain about the applicability of the phrase. At one point he forthrightly contends that the bewildering disillusion of the war experience "affected and would continue to affect the whole national spirit." The writers and artists of the lost generation both reflected and created "the mood of the generation." *The Sun Also Rises*, he asserts, was a "really popular book" with an influence that approached the "universal." Yet Sullivan contradicts his own statement when he writes: "The writers and artists were not the whole of the generation; many, differing in temperament, did not share their emotions during the war, nor after the war share their disillusionment, sense of frustration, and cynicism. Great numbers, an overwhelming majority, indeed practically all of the generation, lived lives normally contented." This contradiction, existing within four pages of *Our Times*, reveals both Sullivan's desire to use the easy generalization implied in "the lost generation" and his awareness that it can be stretched too far.

Sullivan also errs in the direction of excessive emphasis on newness in the 1920s when he treats "The 'Younger Generation.'" The phrase was in wide use after the war and appeared prominently in *Only Yesterday* in connection with the revolution in morals and manners alleged to be taking place. Sullivan has continued this practice. In the course of his discussion he employs Fitzgerald's "all Gods dead" characterization and treats *This Side of Paradise* as a major influence on the conduct of young Americans in the 1920s. Sullivan also attributes too much influence and accuracy to the cartoons of John Held, Jr., the creator of the angular magazine cover flappers and their beaux. Forgetting that these characters were purposely exaggerated and only theoretically representative of a small fraction of American youth, Sullivan declares that "on every street corner was the Held male, buried in a raccoon coat, with patent leather hair, wrinkled socks and bell-bottomed trousers. Frantically bidding for the superior creature's attention was the Held flapper—stubby feet, incredibly long and brittle legs, brief and scanty skirt, two accurate circles of rouge just below the cheek bones, and a tight little felt hat like an inverted tumbler." Five Held couples embellish the page as an illustration. In such statements and such images does the myth of the twenties have its roots.

A few pages later Sullivan dissects the alleged hedonism of the postwar decade. Edna St. Vincent Millay's familiar lines appear:

> My candle burns at both ends;
> It will not last the night;
> But ah, my foes, and oh, my friends,
> It gives a lovely light.

"That," Sullivan comments, "during the early 1920s, could be recited by more young persons than could repeat the formalized codes of more orthodox authorities." Equally effective in making his point is a cartoon reproduced from the *New Yorker* magazine of the mid-twenties. Four flappers are concentrating on a bridge game in a living room; the caption is supplied by a little girl timidly peeking from behind the drapes: "Mother, when you're dummy will you hear my prayers?"

But Sullivan is not always captivated by the froth of the era. In a book that runs to almost seven hundred pages, he makes a number of astute and balanced analyses. He is one of the few to have seen Henry L. Mencken as not primarily a debunker of American civilization but an exponent of many of its most sacred ideals. In a path-breaking chapter on popular music of the 1920s as an expression of thought and emotion, Sullivan argues that, while *Makin' Whoopee* (1928) characterized the "surface" of the twenties, it was *Ol' Man River* (1927) that probed to the "inner soul" of the era with its recognition of frustration and the longing for serenity. Sullivan might have gone on to point out that the frantic whoopee, the lack of restraints, may well have contributed to the inner anxiety that welcomed something enduring and changeless—a river that "jes keeps rollin' along."

In touching upon jazz, however, *Our Times* resumes the theme of rebellion. Defining jazz as "brazen defiance of accepted rules," Sullivan maintains that such a definition "would have served equally well to describe the spirit of much of the generation." And this is the dominant impression that emerges from most of Sullivan's text and illustrations. Change and newness prevailed. As for the "old points of view," they were thrown on "the intellectual scrap-heap as rapidly as old designs of machinery."

There has been no shortage of publicists to carry the Allen-Sullivan view of the twenties on into the present. Indeed the number of books published about the period suggests that this decade has fascinated popularizers of the American past to an unparalleled degree. Americans apparently love either to savor or to lament a time when they imagine, as John Flynn put it in *Scribner's* in 1933, "the flapper, the flivver, Freud and gin ran wild over the land." While little of this writing can be considered intellectual history, it has helped etch a picture of the mood of the 1920s into the national memory.

One comes away from Laurence Greene's *The Era of Wonderful Nonsense* (1939), for instance, with the impression that American civilization in the twenties was obsessed with the trivial, the lurid, and the sadistic. A circulation-hungry press, Greene points out, deserves much of the blame for this emphasis, but the public's appetite, it is implied, is also part of the explanation. Still Greene is able to regard much of the nonsense as wonderful. Not so Henry Morton Robinson. His *Fantastic Interim*, published in 1943, is also a fast-moving, anecdotal popularization which includes the twenties. Robinson, in fact, acknowledges his debt to Frederick Lewis Allen "for blazing a broad and brilliantly lighted trail" and, less eloquently, to Mark Sullivan. But Robinson, writing after the advent of World Waar II, has found it much more difficult to smile at the 1920s than Sullivan, Allen, or Laurence Greene. He fully intends to expose the "ghastly postwar farce" in the hope that he can make its recurrence less likely. Some biographical information inserted into his prologue illuminates Robinson's viewpoint. In 1917 he subscribed wholeheartedly to the Wilsonian war aims and trained Navy recruits to shoot rifles. Then the war came and went and, according to Robinson, people saw "that death—even the most heroic death—solves nothing, guarantees nothing." They also perceived "the land that might have been a field of glory become a crazy quilt of exhibitionism." The resulting bitterness pervades *Fantastic Interim*. One sentence suggests its depth: "political sloth, economic Phariseeism, moral decrepitude, tinseled sentimentality, and brazen Baal-worship wrote a saga of idiocy, signifying nothing." Robinson does not even discern the traditional idealism in the Lindbergh phenomenon—"the whole performance was excessive, pathologic, barbarous—an obscene ritual."

Later popular histories of the 1920s have been less bitter but equally prone to generalization based on dramatic and superficial evidence. In 1947 Lloyd Morris wrote *Postscript to Yesterday*, concerned with "the American mind and heart during the past fifty years." In regard to the twenties Morris has adopted the commonplace interpretation that at the end of World War I "the mood of the American people underwent a drastic change." The result: the collapse of idealism and social reform, cynicism, hedonism, and the advent of gangsters and political scandals. The other parts of the stereotype are also evident in *Postscript to Yesterday*. Collegians were inevitably raccoon-coated and clutching the latest issue of Mencken's *The American Mercury* with the same veneration they accorded their hip flasks. Intellectuals were "adrift" as a result of "the dissolution of the ancestral order." Indeed, Morris is confident that "an intellectual revolution took place between the end of the Great War and the onset of the Great Depression." Its consequences were far reaching: "manners and morals were different. The American cultural heritage was in disrepute. The authority of the past had been broken.... A structure of values, slowly built and long established, had swiftly collapsed. Familiar ideals had the look of 'old illusions that are dead forever.'" This condition, in turn, led to a passion for careless amusement and "the most expensive orgy in history—the 'jazz age.'" A discussion of Fitzgerald follows. Then, predictably, comes Hemingway and his lost generation. Morris, in sum, touches all the bases of the stereotype of the 1920s as it had evolved from Frederick Lewis Allen. And the public responded so enthusiastically that in 1965 Harper and Row issued an attractive paperback edition of Morris's book.

The popularizers have paid particular attention to two social groups of the 1920s—bohemians and bootleggers. Caroline Ware's 1935 description of New York's Greenwich Village is calm and balanced. But later accounts lack the restraint of her *Greenwich Village, 1920–1930*. Allen Churchill's *The Improper Bohemians: A Re-creation of Greenwich Village in Its Heyday* (1959) and Alson J. Smith's *Chicago's Left Bank* (1953) are representative. Without questioning the accuracy of the reporting of Churchill (a prolific free lancer), it is still true that his style deliberately underscores the colorful and wild. The result is a fast-paced, pleasing book, replete with such matters as nude dips in the fountain in Washington Square. Indeed Edna St. Vincent Millay's double-ended candle (see page 10) provides the headquote for one chapter, "The Lost Generation" the title for another. Smith's record of Chicago's bohemia between 1912 and 1924 is also one of prostitutes, poets, and jazz musicians calculated to further the lost generation image. Albert Parry's *Garrets and Pretenders* (1933, paperback edition 1960) deals with both Chicago and New York in the course of its survey of the whole history of American bohemianism.

What Allen Churchill and others have done for the bohemian, Kenneth Allsop does for the bootleggers. His *The Bootleggers and Their Era* (1961) is likewise a highly readable story spiced with photographs of the leading mobsters, both alive and as bullet-punctured corpses. "Scarface" Al Capone emerges from Allsop's pages as "the world's most famous criminal," a figure of truly epic proportions. After reading *The Bootleggers* it is not difficult to see why so many Americans, not to speak of foreign observers, today regard American thought and behavior in the 1920s as little more than a montage of gangland violence. Allsop points this out in an anecdote about a Chicago banker on vacation in the Middle East who happened to mention his home town to a group of Arabs far out on the Egyptian desert. Immediately their "faces lit up and they stuck out their fingers and went 'rat-a-tat-tat' and yelled 'Hah, Alcaponee'!"

The latest contribution to popular accounts of the 1920s is a 1967 imprint, *Babbitts and Bohemians: The American 1920s*, by the biographer Elizabeth Stevenson. Her book is commendable for its awareness that a myth of the twenties exists. The catch phrases describing the decade, she argues in her introductory chapter, have misrepresented it as an "accidental pause in history," full of gangsters, flappers, and self-complacent Babbitts. Yet the rest of the book does not uphold Stevenson's intention of peering beneath the blanket of reputation. Her characterization of the period as "flimsy, juvenile, and doomed" harkens back to Allen, and she quickly becomes victim of the very syndrome she purports to destroy. As its title suggests, *Babbitts and Bohemians* discusses the twenties in terms of caricatures. Abandoning her determination to accept the 1920s "as a pathway of years connected to time before and time after," she falls into the rhetoric of sudden change—"new age" and "new kinds of people." Indeed her analysis is reminiscent of the very chronological mural she promises to avoid.

Conceptions of the past filter into the general consciousness through diverse channels. Anthologies have been another factor in building the reputation of American thought in the twenties. Here, again, the decade has received an inordinate amount of attention. Hoping to capture "the sweet madness" of the years between World War I and the Depression, William Hodapp has edited an extensive collection of fictional selections under the title *The Pleasures of the Jazz Age* (1948). His preface describes the period in astonishing terms: "the Jazz Age was a 'pink-as-a-dream' never-never land suspended in a bubble over the 1920s." Its "Emperor": F. Scott Fitzgerald. And Hodapp seems to believe that the period really was a "ten-year-long week-end party." Fiction only mirrored life in these years when "solid values" disappeared. After such a preface it is understandable that Zane Grey and his fellow tillers of the traditional fields were ruled out of the collection in favor of Fitzgerald and company. Yet, unbelievably, Hodapp accepts the fictional caricatures he presents as "a cross-section of the people who were typical of the times." Perhaps his admitted indebtedness to *Only Yesterday* and *I Remember Distinctly* has shaped this curious notion.

Other editors such as Isabel Leighton with *The Aspirin Age* (1949) and John K. Hutchens in *The American Twenties* (1952) have done their part in keeping attention focused on the "throbbing" (Leighton) quality of the postwar years. However, Hutchens, long-time book reviewer for the *New York Times*, also writes sensitively about the 1920s as a "not-so-delirious" decade. Its writers, he points out, worked long, hard, and seriously at perfecting their art. To be sure, they were disillusioned and dissipated, but this was a "creative disillusion" and a romantic dissipation that inspired great literature. Hutchens forthrightly rejects the term "jazz age" as "foolishly inadequate." As for the twenties being a lost generation, he feels the question is moot. It is certain, however, that the postwar intellectuals "enjoyed enormously the drama of thinking" they were lost and used the self-conception to good artistic advantage in the era's literary flowering. This, Hutchens concludes, "is something to think about when you hear the Twenties discussed as a sort of musical comedy peopled by John Held, Jr. characters playing Mah Jong while resting up between sex-and-gin bouts." In such thinking lies the kernel of new interpretation.

American intellectuals who lived through the 1920s have not been hesitant about exploiting their memories in the form of books about the decade. Indeed many have become better known from their recollections than from their writings at the time. This is certainly true of Malcolm Cowley (Harvard, Class of 1920), one of a group of young American writers who eloped to Paris in the early twenties. Commentators such as Cowley have a great advantage in delineating the 1920s because, if they are honest with themselves, they can distinguish between reputation and reality. Cowley, in general, has had such honesty. His well-known, semiautobiographical *Exile's Return: A Literary Odyssey of the 1920s* was published originally in 1934, reprinted several times, and reissued in a revised paperback edition in 1951. The book was among the first to benefit from the great American curiosity about what happened in those garrets on the Left Bank and in the flats of Greenwich

Village. If they hoped for documentation of debauched and cynical rebellion, the readers of *Exile's Return* must have been disappointed. The book portrays a group of intense writers and poets searching for inspiration and literary guidance. They went to Europe, Cowley declares, "to recover the good life and the traditions of art, to free themselves from organized stupidity, to win their deserved place in the hierarchy of the intellect." They came "in search of values." These, of course, they did not always find, but the impression of the expatriates which Cowley presents in *Exile's Return* differs sharply from that in *The Sun Also Rises.*

Lest his point be missed, Cowley uses the new prologue for the 1951 edition of *Exile's Return* as a way of commenting further on the so-called lost generation. The famous phrase, he decides, is at best a "half-accurate tag." It partially described the minds of a number of young American intellectuals uprooted by the war from country and culture. They experienced "alienation" and, after about a decade, "reintegration"—they returned, physically and spiritually, to America. But while Cowley recognizes the discontent of the intellectuals, he does not make the usual mistake of reading apathy, hedonism, and despair into their lives and thoughts. In the first place the exiles were serious artists. They made a "religion of art" and, at the least, had this antidote to the lost sensation. Second, far from being amoral and valueless, they devoted a considerable part of their energies to a search for certainty. They felt lost, in other words, but wanted to be found. In one of the best, and apparently one of the most easily forgotten, things ever written about the intellectuals of the 1920s, Cowley has said: "the generation belonged to a period of transition from values already fixed to values that had to be created. Its members ... were seceding from the old and yet could adhere to nothing new; they groped their way toward another scheme of life, as yet undefined; in the midst of their doubts and uneasy gestures of defiance they felt homesick for the certainties of childhood."

Fifteen years later, in 1966, Cowley was still engaged in attempting to explain some of the reputation of the twenties. In his introduction to *Fitzgerald and the Jazz Age*, which he edited with Robert Cowley as a research anthology for college students, he rejects his earlier adjective, "alienated," for "disillusioned" or "disenchanted." But he goes beyond label making to analysis. Disillusion, in Cowley's reappraisal, means specifically loss of faith in social reform and progress. Postwar Americans had not been disillusioned or lost in other senses. "They committed themselves to various personal goals—success in business, or escape from business into the world of art, of achieving grace under pressure, or acquiring a wealth of experience, or simply having a good time—in the same desperate fashion that young men of other generations have committed themselves to social or religious or political ideals. In a sense," Cowley concludes, "they too were living in an age of faith." Still, for those who passed over his introduction, the selections in *Fitzgerald and the Jazz Age* make it easy to resurrect the old images: Frederick Lewis Allen, Mark Sullivan, Fitzgerald, Mencken, and Hemingway are all represented, along with material concerning the flapper, flaming youth, gangsters, and booze.

The sheer quantity of memoirs from the pens of those who lived through the 1920s has added an important layer to the reputation of these years. A handful of intellectuals, writing largely about each other, have created the impression that every thinking American in the early twenties either sought exile in Paris or wished he could. Some like Matthew Josephson in *Life Among the Surrealists* (1962) first protest the lost generation appellation but then proceed to document what they disclaim. Sexuality of diverse varieties, alcoholism, and wild parties, after all, make for a more interesting book than a description of trying to write stories and poems in cheap, cold water flats. And so the myth survives. Samuel Putnam includes the intriguing subtitle "Memoirs of a Lost and Found Generation" in his *Paris Was Our Mistress* (1947) but then allows the question to drop. In *We Were Interrupted* (1947) Burton Rascoe first brands labels like "The Fantastic Interim," "Jazz Age," and "Age of Wild and Flaming Youth" as "superficial"; then he uses the most hackneyed of all, "The Roaring Twenties," as a chapter title. Rascoe's frontispiece, moreover, features a willowly and totally nude flapper dancing on a table amidst balloons, streamers, and cocktail-sipping couples. His Parisian interlude also merits a chapter, of course. Yet in his epilogue Rascoe writes with wisdom. The twenties, he declares, meant revolt against restrictions and conventions but not "mental confusion, cynicism, and ethical anarchy." A "slight shift of emphasis on values" occurred similar to a change in style of dress. Commentators had exaggerated the change, forgetting "the French axiom that a happy marriage has no history" and the newspaper adage that it is only news when man bites dog. Rascoe concludes that the 1920s had "hearts as steady, illusions as fixed, principles as sound (and as flexible), faith as high, and a sense of obligation as tenacious as those of any generation that preceded it."

Publishers have seemed to be eager for any memoir concerning Americans in Paris during the 1920s. Among the many lesser accounts, Caresse Crosby's *The Passionate Years* (1955) is notable chiefly for the swinging life its author led on two continents and her marriage to the suicide Harry Crosby. Morley Callaghan's *That Summer in Paris* (1963) has the marketable subtitle, "Memories of Tangled Friendships with Hemingway, Fitzgerald, and Some Others." Several cuts above these books is Ernest Hemingway's *A Moveable Feast: Sketches of the Author's Life in Paris in the Twenties,* published in 1964 to front page reviews and substantial sales. The American appetite for the lost generation myth apparently had not dulled in the thirty-eight years since *The Sun Also Rises;* the same kinds of people drift through both books. Indeed as recently as 1968 the Paris memoirs of the minor expatriate writer Robert McAlmon were reissued for the first time in the United States and received enthusiastic front page treatment in the book review section of the *New York Times.*

In the category of reminiscences are two semiautobiographical novels by the Fitzgeralds: Scott's *Tender Is the Night* (1934) and Zelda's *Save Me the Waltz* (1932). Understandably distorted, since they purport to document the destruction of each person by the other, they have nonetheless been taken into the minds and hearts of many Americans, along with the entire Fitzgerald legend, as an accurate representation of how it really was with Americans on the Continent in the twenties. The dramatic manner in which Fitzgerald played out his life added further fuel to the cult. And then the books began: in 1945 Edmund Wilson's edited collection of Fitzgerald's later stories, letters, and notebooks under the title *The Crack-Up;* in 1950 Budd Schulberg's *The Disenchanted,* portraying Fitzgerald's decline and fall in fictional form; a year later Arthur Mizener's *The Far Side of Paradise: A Biography of F. Scott Fitzgerald;* and in 1963 Andrew Turnbull's massive, edited *The Letters of F. Scott Fitzgerald.* Nearly all of Fitzgerald's novels have recent paperback editions and a host of eager scholarly interpreters. As a result Fitzgerald and the 1920s are so closely linked in the American mind that the individual, so to speak, wags the decade.

The roar of the 1920s was eminently photographable, and the photograph has been a major tool in the construction of the decade's reputation. Mark Sullivan pioneered in 1935 when he presented visual evidence, including cartoons and stills from motion pictures, in Volume VI of *Our Times*. In 1947 the Allens' *I Remember Distinctly* (see page 8) launched the era of the lavishly-illustrated historical spectacular. Ten years later a New York newspaper editor named Paul Sann published a pictorial history of the twenties entitled *The Lawless Decade*. It enjoyed nine printings in the next ten years. Explaining his title, Sann has written that "the great postwar shocks of the twenties left very little sacred and very little unturned; most of the old playing rules were rewritten." Laws both moral and civil were "ground into the dust" at this time; "the old gods fell, the old traditions cracked." The pictures and commentary that follow support Sann's generalizations. *The Lawless Decade* is a visual *Only Yesterday*. All the familiar elements are present, from the bathing beauties to the bread lines. The text does little but explain the illustrations, yet the effect of the whole is to leave the reader with the impression that only sensational and scandalous things happened in the 1920s.

Three other recent volumes have used both visual and written evidence to recreate the twenties. *Vanity Fair: Selections from America's Most Memorable Magazine: A Cavalcade of the 1920s and 1930s*, edited by Cleveland Amory and Frederic Bradlee, appeared in a lavish format in 1960. More sophisticated than *The Lawless Decade* and compiled from the files of a single periodical, the book still gives the impression that the twenties were a gay whirl of careless and beautiful people. Notwithstanding Bruce Catton's essay to the contrary, *American Heritage* magazine's special edition, *The Twenties* (August, 1965), also stresses the surface of the decade. Catton, however, recognizes that everybody did not do "fantastic things" between 1920 and 1930. In his opinion most Americans "were serious, hard-working people who did their best to earn a living, bring up their children, live decently by the best light they had, and lay away a few dollars for their old age." Yet, surprisingly, Catton accepts the idea of the twenties "as an empty place between two eras, with old familiar certainties and hopes drifting off like mist and new ones not yet formulated." Finally, *The Revealing Eye: Personalities of the 1920's* with photographs by

Nickolas Muray and words by Paul Gallico (1967) reveals that American publishers believe the public appetite for the fabulousness of the 1920s to be unsatiated.

A subject as juicy as the 1920s could not for long avoid treatment by the recording and motion picture industries. In 1950 Edward R. Murrow compiled a record album, *I Can Hear It Now, 1919–1949: 30 Years of Audible History.* The portion concerning the 1920s follows the accustomed pattern. Between tapes or reconstructions of the famous voices of the decade, Murrow interjects analysis such as "the people were hot, hyperthyroid and roaring" in reference to 1925. No one really cared about enforcing prohibition, Murrow notes, and "besides, these were the Roaring Twenties, and it was more important to know what Consolidated Can closed at and would Shipwreck Kelly break the flagpole-sitting record." On such an unbalanced diet have innumerable high school and college students of American history been dutifully fed.

Another favorite classroom aid has been McGraw-Hill's text film, *A Chronicle of America's Jazz Age.* Frederick Lewis Allen was one of its creators, and in the Allen manner the film underscores the thrills and frills of the time. "You could," the narrator declares, "whip up a Charleston contest anywhere in the country." Viewers are told that after World War I Americans experienced "a new kind of world," "a new age." McGraw-Hill's film strip, *Roaring Twenties,* and Guidance Associates' *Reckless Years: 1919–29* follow the same format.

Unquestionably television has been a major influence in shaping the image of the 1920s. In 1958 *The Untouchables* made its debut in the Desilu Playhouse series with two one-hour shows. The following year this account of prohibition agents versus gangsters in the Chicago underworld became a prime time series in its own right, and it enjoyed an immense following among viewers of all ages for the next four years. In its peak months (January and February 1961) the rating services estimated its audience at thirty million persons. While carefully authentic in its attention to details like cars, clothes, and other props, *The Untouchables* has had the unfortunate effect of leading a generation of viewers to believe that the American 1920s were synonymous with Elliott Ness, Al Capone, sawed-off shotguns, and cars careening through plate glass windows. Several more shows featuring the twenties rode the wake of *The Untouchables'* popularity. *The Lawless Years, Pete Kelly's Blues,* and *The Roaring Twenties* have underscored the idea of a wild, tumultuous decade. So have Hollywood-produced films such as the story of gambler Arnold Rothstein, *King of the Roaring 20's,* whose advertisements promised a portrayal of "The Golden Years of the Jazz Mad Era." Another recent motion picture, *Thoroughly Modern Millie,* conveys the same message.

Professionals

Compared to the number of popularizers of the 1920s, the amount of professional scholarship dealing broadly with the thought of the decade is still slight. Even when they have dealt with the 1920s, historians have found it difficult to escape the looming shadow of the decade's popular reputation.

The first professional to write about the twenties, however, had no such problem. William Preston Slossen's *The Great Crusade and After, 1914–1928* appeared in 1930, a year before *Only Yesterday.* Slossen, for forty years a professor at the University of Michigan, has distinguished two main tendencies in American thought after World War I. The first was "cynicism and disillusionment" that made a jest of "ancient ideals" and produced a vogue of debunking. Mencken, of course, was its high priest. Second, Slossen has seen a "remarkable intensification of nationalism" in the postwar American mind, especially on the popular level. Although this often produced intolerant and hysterical behavior, Slossen rightly identifies it as sincere patriotism, "almost religious in strength and character."

James Truslow Adams, one of the last of the great gentleman historians in the United States, belongs in the company of Frederick Lewis Allen and Mark Sullivan as an important early influence on attitudes toward the twenties. After a career in finance and business, he retired to a small Connecticut village and leisurely began to write history. His first important volume, *The Founding of New England* (1921), won the Pulitzer Prize. In 1932 he had the distinction of having two of his works appear on the list of best-selling nonfiction: *The Epic of America* was first; *The March of Democracy,* seventh. Adams writes political rather than intellectual history, but he also takes some account of national thought. In *The Epic* he lashes out at the postwar American spirit, asserting that a comparison of the country in 1931 with that of 1912 indicates a long slip backwards. Specifically, the idealism of the time of Wilson and the first Roosevelt had vanished. Taking its place as the dynamic of American history were recklessness and material greed. What Adams calls "the American dream" of creating a better man, a better civilization, had given way to pursuit of the dollar and "cheap amusements." Moreover, we were losing the tradition of individualism. *The March* (the second volume of which, including the section on the 1920s, was published in 1933) also bears the clear mark of having been written after the Crash. Adams adds a new name for the 1920s, "The Mad Decade," and portrays Americans of that time as obsessed by a "pathological unrest and mental panic" which resulted, for one thing, in the hysterical persecution of aliens. "Genuine Americanism" was horribly distorted. Toward the end of the decade, Adams alleges, Americans suffered from blind delirium in believing they could defy economic laws.

While Adams' books of the early 1930s support the idea of the 1920s as an unfortunate interlude in the history of the American spirit, his *The American: The Making of a New Man* of 1943 strikes a different note. The volume purports to study the national character and consequently pays more attention to intellectual history. Near the end of *The American* Adams has inserted a remarkable passage on the 1920s, one that contradicts the analyses of Allen and Sullivan, as well as some of Adams' own earlier ideas. The thought and behavior of Americans in the twenties, it seems to Adams, "indicated a desperate desire to recapture an earlier America." People yearned for the simpler past of farms and kerosene lamps; hence the popularity of the homespun Calvin Coolidge. Such homesickness for American origins did not reflect a desire to turn back the clock, according to Adams, but it was "in their blood and doing something to them." Could not the speculative mania of the 1920s, Adams wonders, be seen as "a defiant demonstration of the old free-for-all struggle for gain, individualism, the take-a-chance urge, on the frontier." Americans of the twenties, Adams concludes, were vaguely but persistently "reaching back to the various phases of the America of the past, trying somehow to find release from a world which had got a bit too complicated, and to 'regain the first fine careless rapture' of what they felt they *had* been." Perhaps the fact that James Truslow Adams was a student of the entire American experience, rather than of the very recent past, as were Allen and Sullivan, explains his ability to discern continuity as well as change in the values of the twenties.

With the advent of intellectual history as a distinct discipline after 1940, historians have paid increasing attention to the temper of the postwar years. Some, like Ralph Henry Gabriel and Stow Persons, do not elect to discuss the 1920s as a separate period. In emphasizing the continuity of American ideas since at least the Civil War they have done the historiography of thought in the 1920s a signal service. Merle Curti's Pulitzer Prize-winning *The Growth of American Thought* (1943) also recognizes that "many of the attitudes commonly assumed to be new in the 1920s...had appeared before the war." For some intellectuals of the twenties cynical disillusionment and haunting uncertainty were the dominant mode; yet, Curti points out, others engaged in a restatement of the genteel tradition. As for "the mass of ordinary people," such matters were of little if any concern. Consequently, Curti implies, generalizations about a wasteland and hollow men ring hollow themselves.

Another landmark in American intellectual history was the publication in 1950 of Henry Steele Commager's *The American Mind*. Commager is adept at picking out threads of thought and tracing them through time. His chapters on innovation and tradition in literature span American history from the 1890s through the 1930s. Balance marks these pages, but when Commager turns to the 1920s even he oversimplifies. "The twenties brought cynicism and disillusionment," we are told; there were no reform crusades on the Lord's behalf because intellectuals "did not believe in the Lord." Instead they "fled to Greenwich Village or to the Left Bank and thumbed their noses at the middle classes or at Puritanism or at the small town." Fitzgerald, Commager concludes, spoke for a lost generation.

In 1956 Henry May published, "Shifting Perspectives on the 1920's," in the *Mississippi Valley Historical Review*. The paper concerns the ways in which Americans have regarded that decade in the intervening quarter century, and it suggests that the reputation of the 1920s was more a commentary on later generations than on the twenties themselves. Depending on the point of observation and the observer's frame of mind, the alleged irresponsibility of the postwar years was either deplorable or attractive. "It seems clear," May has concluded, "that one cannot say much about the twenties as a disintegration or revolution without giving more attention to the old regime, the presumed prewar agreement." Accordingly May published *The End of American Innocence: A Study of the First*

Years of Our Own Time, 1912–1917 in 1959. Its central point is that American intellectuals revolted against the ideas and values of the nineteenth century and that the essentials of this "cultural revolution" occurred not in the 1920s as a result of the war but in the five years preceding American intervention. World War I and the bungled peace only accelerated and embittered an attack on the old standards that was already under way. The book, then, does not reject the idea of a watershed in American intellectual history; it only moves it back half a decade. May, moreover, does not alter the image of the twenties as a time of cynicism and disillusion; he only changes the explanation of how it became lost.

The End of American Innocence is one of the most important studies of intellectual history in the early twentieth century. Its shortcomings, therefore, are important as well. One is May's tendency to extend his generalizations beyond the support of his evidence. Had he contented himself with the detailed description and analysis of American writing, poetry, and art between 1912 and 1917 that forms the bulk of his book, there would be little to contest. This is superb intellectual history. But May has made bold to extrapolate from his handful of intellectuals an explanation of the *national* temper. His title leads with its chin. The absence of guilt, doubt, and complexity (what May terms "innocence") simply did not end for many Americans either between 1912 and 1917, or in the 1920s, or since. May, to be sure, is not writing about common people, but that is only a better reason why he should have qualified his thesis. Once only does he admit that parts of the old innocence did "survive in different form, and some Americans still held to it all." Yet the tone of the rest of the book makes this admission seem grudging. Indeed, in the next sentence May contends that the sureness with which "Americans" believed in innocence is "long gone."

In his concern for delineating watersheds in the history of ideas, May ignores the fact that intellectuals, like other people, are often ambivalent and contradictory—simultaneously attacking and defending innocence, for instance. Is it ever wise when dealing with ideas to use such concepts as "dividing line," "barrier," "revolution," and "end" as May does? Granted that authors usually have little choice in such matters, can a book cover be defended that features a symbolic tree, verdant on one side and stark dead on the other, such as that which adorned May's paperback edition? Moreover, why does May choose 1912–1917 as the end of national innocence? Surely champions could be found for 1861–1865, or for 1607–1612 when the Jamestowners had their innocent expectations of wealth and ease shattered by the harsh realities of a wilderness condition. Others might contend that the old credo never died. If patterns must be drawn, perhaps the best would represent American innocence as passing through a series of half-finished cycles, rising only to fall by the weight of its own overoptimistic expectations.

Four years after publishing *The End of American Innocence*, Henry May again reviewed American thought in the 1920s in an edited pamphlet designed for college courses, *The Discontent of the Intellectuals: A Problem of the Twenties* (1963). While focusing on the disgruntled American intellectuals, May is aware that they stood apart from the mainstream. An "optimistic majority" also existed.

World War I, according to May's introductory commentary in *The Discontent*, "made . . . fundamental questioning of prevailing American beliefs much more common." The intellectuals in the twenties spiraled downward in a whirlwind of resentment of and alienation from American civilization. He does concede, however, that degrees of alienation existed in the 1920s and that only the blackest entailed "a wholesale rejection of the values which had dominated American society since the beginning." He also concedes that, toward the conclusion of the 1920s, alienation began to lose its hold as Americans searched for values and credos. With this idea May opens a window for reinterpreting the earlier part of the decade as well. Yet in his concluding pages he reverts to the stereotype, assuming intellectuals *were* alienated from America and asking, in a chapter title, "How Did They Get That Way?" A more fruitful approach would have omitted the "How."

Other historians have dealt with the problem of the American mind in the 1920s in diverse ways. Many have accepted the stereotype without qualification. In discussing the war guilt question, Selig Adler, for instance, simply assumes that one must "turn to the *Zeitgeist* of the 'jazz age.' The new and the bizarre had strong appeal to the individualism of the 'lost generation.'" Arthur Schlesinger, Jr., in his *The Crisis of the Old Order, 1919–1933*, Volume I in *The Age of Roosevelt*, accepts Fitzgerald as the spokesman of the new generation and quotes the "all Gods dead" statement as evidence. For Schlesinger, who was delineating the scene upon which Franklin D. Roosevelt was to emerge, the 1920s were marked by "the exhaustion of liberalism" and "the revolt of the intellectuals" from reform ideals. In the editors' introduction to John D. Hicks' *Republican Ascendency, 1921–1933* (1960), Henry Steele Commager and Richard B. Morris take up the interregnum theme by branding the twenties a "Sargasso Sea" between Wilsonian idealism and the New Deal. William Leuchtenburg's widely used *The Perils of Prosperity, 1914–1932* (1958) sees these years as a time when old guidelines "broke down." An exciting writer, Leuchtenburg integrates most of the well-worn lost generation quotations and roaring twenties anecdotes in his account, and from it they have been extracted by countless college lecturers. Leuchtenburg's book is reminiscent of *Only Yesterday*. His ninth chapter is entitled "The Revolution in Morals," as Allen's fifth is "The Revolution in Manners and Morals." Allen's quotation from a newspaper advertisement for a motion picture—"brilliant men, beautiful jazz babies, champagne baths, midnight revels, petting parties in the purple dawn, all ending in one terrific smashing climax that makes you gasp"—Leuchtenburg also uses. "The disintegration of traditional American values— so sharply recorded by novelists and artists," he concludes, "was reflected in a change in manners and morals that shook American society to its depths."

Leuchtenburg also subscribes to the view that the war and the 1920s killed progressivism. This opinion was widespread in writings on American history until the publication, in 1959 in the *American Historical Review*, of Arthur S. Link's seminal paper, "What Happened to the Progressive Movement in the 1920s?" Link suggests that there was considerably more Progressive energy in the 1920s than was hitherto supposed. Equally significant in revising the reputation of the 1920s has been John W. Ward's "The Meaning of Lindbergh's Flight," in *American Quarterly* for 1958, which has revealed an underlying hunger in American society for old-time values and virtues, a nostalgia quite out of keeping with the dominant reputation of the twenties.

By the 1960s most professionals writing about the 1920s were handling the stereotype cautiously. "To judge from some accounts," David A. Shannon caustically remarks, "Americans did little else from 1920 to 1929 but make millions in the stock market, dance the Charleston and the Black Bottom, dodge gangster bullets, wear raccoon coats, and carry hip flasks." Terming this view "shallow and exaggerated" and its proponents "a little giddy," Shannon does his best to paint a calmer and more accurate picture in *Between the Wars: America, 1919–1941* (1965). The intellectual rebels, Shannon warns, must not be taken as representing the great majority of Americans whose lives and thoughts were much the same as before. Morrell Heald makes the same point on a more abstract level with his interpretation of the twenties as "a troubled decade in which old and new were inextricably intermingled." Discarding the notion of rebellion, Heald stresses uncertainty and fear of change as the decade's main themes.

Paul A. Carter is also skeptical about the accuracy of labels like "jazz age" and "lost generation." While not primarily concerned with intellectual history, his *The Twenties in America* (1968) raises doubts about the rebellion of the young and the despair of the lost. Carter's interpretation of the 1920s as a time of tension (between urban and rural values, for instance) rather than a new era may be found in the work of other recent historians. George E. Mowry, for example, writes in *The Twenties: Fords, Flappers & Fanatics* (1963) that "societies do not give up the old ideals and attitudes easily; the conflicts between the representatives of the older elements of traditional American culture and the prophets of the new day were at times as bitter as they were extensive." Mowry's edited anthology is intended to illustrate this cultural conflict rather than to document an intellectual revolution, and in so doing it performs a sorely needed service. In their introduction to another anthology of American thought, Gerald N. Grob and George A. Billias question the stereotype of the 1920s so far as to imply that the decade should *not* be considered as a unified and unique epoch in American history.

The most recent professional works on the 1920s also reveal the approach of a new, more balanced understanding. John Braeman, Robert H. Bremner, and David Brody, who together edited *Change and Continuity in Twentieth-Century America: The 1920's* (1968), have presented essays which demonstrate that both the forces mentioned in their title were at work on the thought of the age. The contributors to the volume show that, in the area of ideas, experimentation was countered by a vigorous conservatism. Milton Plesur, editor of a 1969 collection of readings entitled *The 1920's*, finds it difficult to break away from the impression that the period was "an age of ballyhoo with a 'Hellzapoppin' attitude toward life," that *Makin' Whoopee* was a song which "mirrored the age," and that intellectuals were completely alienated. Elsewhere, however, Plesur describes a problematic age replete with "incongruities" and "paradoxes." Most young Americans, he thinks, never visited a speakeasy and could not be described by quoting from F. Scott Fitzgerald. The revolt of angry youth, Plesur believes, was "more a fad than a true revolution." And yet his choice for a reading on manners and morals is a selection from *Only Yesterday* which begins: "A first-class revolt against the accepted American order was certainly taking place."

Literary critics and literary historians, whose approach in many cases is closely related to that of intellectual historians, have had an important role in shaping the reputation of the twenties. After an initial period of finger-shaking deprecation during the 1930s, it has become commonplace to celebrate the 1920s as a time of literary flowering. Scholars love to tick off the names of the great who began to write between World War I and the Depression. They also appear to agree that the existence of a lost generation—particularly its rebelliousness—was somehow responsible for the creative impulse of the twenties. In *On Native Grounds: A Study of American Prose Literature from 1890 to the Present* (1942), Alfred Kazin uses Fitzgerald's "all Gods dead" pronouncement to make the point. Robert E. Spiller, *et al.*, *Literary History of the United States* (originally 1946) also uses it along with the lost generation idea. *This Side of Paradise,* Spiller's team confidently declares, was "the generation's masculine primer," while Edna St. Vincent Millay's poems served as the ladies', and *The Sun Also Rises* was "a second reader for both sexes."

The Twenties: American Writing in the Postwar Decade (1955, revised edition 1962) by Frederick J. Hoffman is the single most important book in its field. While aware that the decade has not been "fairly portrayed" by the popularizers as well as by previous scholars, Hoffman still accepts the essentials of the revolt and rejection view of American intellectuals. "The 1920s," he declares, "were marked by a disrespect for tradition," a negativism, and an "attitude of refusal." But Hoffman's method is sufficiently sophisticated to admit exceptions and qualifications. Thus, he devotes an entire chapter to "Forms of Traditionalism" in the literature of the 1920s. Willa Cather, for instance, is identified not as a debunker but as one nervously clutching for values and ethics in the American past. Likewise the new humanists and the fugitive agrarians are seen as standing apart from "the pattern of rejection" to which many of their fellow writers adhered. Throughout *The Twenties* Hoffman emphasizes the seriousness of the literary endeavor in these years. He condemns those who have led the public to believe that the writers of the 1920s were irresponsible and dissipated adolescents. Fitzgerald, he points out, was not just the chronicler of flaming youth but a great writer. In his conclusion, Hoffman represents the intellectuals of the twenties as naive rather than lost. It was not that they had no guidelines but rather that "they were open to every new influence that came along." The central tenet of their faith was a belief in the value of experimentation in their lives and in their art. They rebelled, in other words, only to rebuild.

American literary historians since Hoffman have continued his attack on the myth of a lost generation. In an essay in Robert Spiller, ed., *A Time of Harvest: American Literature, 1910–1960* (1962), Arthur Mizener addresses the question directly: "the 'Lost Generation' is a somewhat misleading name . . . , as perhaps a name that reflects the judgment of an age on itself always is." Seeing through the fashionable posture of disillusion and despair prevalent at the time, Mizener goes on to explain that the writers of the 1920s were joyful and optimistic pioneers. Theirs was a vision of remaking American literature and American life. "If they were lost," he asserts, "they were lost as explorers are, not as the damned are." Archibald MacLeish has also attacked the stale ideas associated with the lost generation interpretation. Writing in the *Saturday Review* in 1966, he declares that "it was not the Lost Generation which was lost: It was the world out of which that generation came." Consequently the intellectuals were not so much bewildered as challenged and inspired. The results are apparent in the literature of the twenties which, according to MacLeish, could be defended as "the greatest period of literary and artistic innovation since the Renaissance." Probing further along this vein, Richard E. Langford and William E. Taylor in their edited *The Twenties: Poetry and Prose* (1966) and John Killinger in *Hemingway and the Dead Gods* (1960) identify the beginnings of existentialism, in form if not yet in name, in the so-called lost generation. "There was nothing 'lost,'" write Langford and Taylor, "about a generation of writers such as these. . . . Behind the despair, beneath the whimper, lies the search for personal meaning."

If textbooks in American history are reflectors of the profession's collective judgment on the thought of the 1920s, then the challenge to the stereotype, evident in some of the recent scholarship, has not made much headway. With few exceptions the texts accept the myths of the jazz age and the lost generation without qualification. So standardized is the treatment of the 1920s, in fact, that a composite portrait can be drawn: The typical text begins with a chapter or section entitled "Those Golden Twenties" or, perhaps, "The Roaring Twenties." Then follows a generalized statement such as "idealism gave way to materialism, naiveté to cynicism, moral purposefulness to irresponsibility, progressivism to reaction, community spirit to rugged individualism, faith to iconoclasm." There is a tendency to lump all Americans together: "the people of the United States, suffering the hangover from a moralistic binge, cut loose from idealism and became part of what Gertrude Stein has called 'the Lost Generation.'" Students are told that Americans responded in three ways: they became alienated from and revolted against their civilization, fleeing to join the expatriates in Paris; they plunged wholeheartedly into the pursuit of the dollar, becoming Babbitts; they indulged in a careless search for pleasure, creating the jazz age or the "era of flaming youth."

The usual textbook continues with a series of supporting statements. Fitzgerald's "all Gods dead" statement (page 7) invariably appears. Indeed it seems among the most heavily-fired quotations in the text writers' entire arsenal. Fitzgerald himself is said to mirror the spirit of the twenties both in his literature and his life. Only slightly less popular as quotations are Millay's quatrain (page 10), Hemingway's rejection of idealism (page 9), and T. S. Eliot's expressions of a "wasteland" inhabited by "hollow men." The "petting parties in the purple dawn" quotation (page 26) that Frederick Lewis Allen bequeathed to the profession appears in several books. Mencken is usually mentioned in connection with the alleged iconoclasm of the time. On the popular level the supposed obsession with trivia is underscored: "it was a decade of tinsel, bright lights, flappers, bathing-beauty contests, and gang wars over bootlegging. It was an unreal world of nonsense that died in the stock-market crash of 1929." Understandably the typical text concludes with suggestions for further reading in which Allen's *Only Yesterday* is featured. The older texts generally depict the 1920s as a tragic interlude: "seldom did a generation bequeath so little that was permanent, so much that was troublesome, to the future." The newer ones are apt to recognize at least the literary flowering of the time.

Some of the more recent authors of textbooks attempt to think independently of the common reputation of the 1920s. One of the leading high school texts, *Rise of the American Nation* by Lewis Paul Todd and Merle Curti, recognizes that "people's ideas, beliefs, and everyday habits did not suddenly change as though by some stroke of magic on Armistice Day in 1918." Frank Freidel, David Shannon, John R. Alden, and a few others point out in their texts that the sensational surface of the twenties has obscured the fact that most Americans led "sober, quiet lives" in these years. Several authors take pains to describe the persistence of the Progressive mentality after World War I and the intensification of nationalism among the masses. Oscar Handlin's *The History of the United States* (1968) identifies these patriots as "people who yearned for the old morality" and were shocked at the breakdown of the "old standards." In *The Torch is Passed* (1968) Forrest McDonald employs all the familiar components of the stereotype and yet recognizes that, "if you asked a typical southern farm youth what he had done during the Jazz Age, he could only reply that he plowed and slopped the hogs and did the chores, for that was all there was to do and all he knew how to do." Frederick Lewis Allen, in McDonald's estimation, is in many respects "highly misleading and superficial."

In the main, however, Allen and his colleagues have prevailed. The revision of the reputation of the 1920s as they created it is in its infancy so far as textbooks are concerned. Most students must come away from courses in American history believing that the twenties were truly a strange interlude.

Three facts emerge from a survey of the reputation of American thought between the end of World War I and the beginning of the Great Depression. These years, first of all, have received more publicity, more popular attention, than any other decade-length period in the American past. Second, the twenties have generally been discussed as an interregnum, clearly separated from the progressivism and the war, on the one hand, and from the Depression and New Deal on the other. In the third place, American life and thought in the 1920s has been stereotyped to such an extent that certain limited but highly visible aspects have colored the whole. What was new has been blown up out of all proportion to what was not. Yet the deep ruts that the stereotype has worn in American thinking about the twenties are not easily avoided. Even those who know better have found it difficult to conceive of these years as other than a lost generation or a jazz age. Few areas of American historiography better sustain Voltaire in his conception of the historian as magician.

Chapter 3

Intellectuals: A Lost Generation?

War

The outbreak of war among the European powers in the summer of 1914 caught American intellectuals by complete surprise. Along with most thoughtful men in the West, they believed that, as part of the world's foremost civilization at an optimum time in history, they were beyond such dangerous and antiquated practices as total war. The shock was especially strong in the United States where belief in the possibility of a better life was a major component of the national creed. Specifically, Americans subscribed to the idea of mission: that the New World origins of the country had given it a special responsibility and a superior ability to lead mankind toward perfection. We led, according to the official faith, by setting a good example. John Winthrop's reference to America as a city on a hill, attracting the world's admiring glance, has been quoted and emulated so frequently because it catches the essence of what Americans like to believe about themselves. Originally conceived of in sacred terms in reference to a godly society, the emphasis of the American mission had gradually shifted in a secular direction toward individual liberty and material well-being. Service to man, rather than to God, became the new purpose. And in 1914, at the conclusion of a period of unprecedented material growth and, more immediately, of domestic reform, it appeared that the millennium was at least closer.

As self-appointed custodians of ideals and fundamental moral principles, pre-1910 American intellectuals believed it their responsibility to lead the nation upward and onward. If there were obstacles to be overcome, intellectuals sounded the call and led the reformers' charge. If idealistic visions were the requirement, they provided blueprints for utopias. The twentieth century began with most intellectuals in the United States sanguine about the future of the Western world. The wave of pride and confidence generated by the Renaissance and the Enlightenment still rolled strongly. What a work of art was man! His intellect, disciplined with science, seemed capable of explaining and utilizing every natural process. And the same natural laws that provided the key to the physical world were thought to make possible a social science as well. With liberal application of the oil of natural rights, most Americans confidently expected the social vehicle to run squeakless forever.

World War I. exploded this halcyon vision. Instead of reasoning out their difficulties, nations assumed to be the world's most advanced had turned to the troglodytic method of bashing each other over the head. Centuries of progress seemed to be wiped out at a stroke. The European belligerents, according to the *New York Times* of August 2, 1914, seemed to "have reverted to the condition of savage tribes roaming the forests and falling upon each other in a fury of blood and carnage to achieve the ambitious designs of chieftains clad in skins and drunk with mead." Americans of intellect, engaged at the time in an attempt to advance social justice through the Progressive movement, were stunned.

If the commencement of fighting in Europe in 1914 shocked American intellectuals, the spectacle of their own country entering the conflict three years later should have left them aghast. In fact, and in general, it did not. The concept of mission, which had proven malleable enough to cover the Mexican and the Spanish-American wars, sufficed to justify intervention. Joining the side of Great Britain and France, it was argued, would further the ideals of freedom and peace. As Woodrow Wilson put it, war would make the world "safe for democracy" and "make similar wars impossible." Indisputably an intellectual (he held the Ph.D. and had been president of Princeton), Wilson succeeded in channeling the energies of the Progressive movement into the war effort. He contended that America's custodianship of liberty and justice did not stop at the national boundary. Having pursued these ideals on the local, state, and federal levels, the next step was obvious. After political and economic "bosses," the war lords of the world! The national mission entailed defending American ideals wherever they were threatened.

Initially most intellectuals accepted this logic and supported not only the war effort abroad but hysterical superpatriotism at home. Apparently intellect was no antidote to propaganda. Some scholars, especially economists and political scientists, left their academic jobs and went to Washington, D.C., to give of their expertise. Many others used pen and voice to vindicate American intervention. Few had more influence in this respect than John Dewey, a philosopher whose prewar writing had emphasized the possibility and the desirability of reaching peaceful, rational solutions to social problems. Since the 1880s Dewey had been developing a pragmatic position from which ideas and actions could be evaluated according to their usefulness in forging a better world. Dewey's central point, expressed for instance in *Creative Intelligence* (1917, but three months before intervention), was that the observation of the practical consequences of believing in an idea should determine its value. The scientific method, not force, should be the basis of belief.

Seemingly John Dewey should have opposed American participation in the European war. Yet, immediately following our April 1917 entrance into that conflict, he published a series of articles in *New Republic* arguing that war and his variety of pragmatism were compatible. Pacifism, Dewey argued, was an outgrowth of moral training that "emphasizes the emotions rather than intelligence, ideals rather than specific purposes, the nurture of personal motives rather than the creation of social agencies and environments." The European war, however, was a specific situation that demanded a specific, practical response on the part of the United States. "A somewhat mushy belief in the existence of disembodied moral forces," according to Dewey, would not "bring about what is right." Instead concrete action had to be taken, and in "the light of objective facts," only force would create a just and permanent peace. Dewey advised those who objected to war on conscience and principle to follow the "skillful" leadership of President Wilson who understood the necessity of war at the same time he deplored it.

In June 1918 Dewey published "What Are We Fighting For?" in

the *Independent*. Later retitled "The Social Possibilities of War," the essay expressed another reason for his support of intervention. The general state of emergency and its accompanying spirit of private sacrifice for public ends, he pointed out, would hasten the advent of the socialization of the means of production and distribution. For Dewey this was a desirable consequence. The central government's control over the private sector of the economy would bring about the kind of social and economic justice for which the Progressives had labored with only partial success. The end result of the mobilization effort would be a permanent "democratization of industry." American liberalism, as Dewey defined it, would be immeasurably advanced. The war, then, fitted easily into Dewey's pragmatism as an instrument of social usefulness.

It is safe to say that most American intellectuals followed Dewey's reasoning in attempting to explain how a wrong could so suddenly become a right. One notable exception, however, was Randolph Bourne. Initially ignored in his protests against intervention, Bourne (he died shortly after the Armistice in 1918, at the age of thirty-two) and his writing gained increasing recognition as the aftermath of the war proved his pessimistic expectations correct. Intellectuals began to find in his work an articulation of their second thoughts. Yet Bourne never succumbed to that nihilistic despair alleged to be characteristic of the lost generation. His mind is an excellent starting point for examining the war and the intellectuals.

As much as any American of the decade 1910–1920 Bourne deserves the designation "intellectual." Exceptionally bright (he could read at the age of two), he early in life developed a double curvature of the spine which necessitated his emphasizing mental rather than physical achievement. Bourne enrolled at Princeton in 1903, dropped out for want of money, and, after a hiatus of six years, entered Columbia University. There he came under the influence of Charles A. Beard, James Harvey Robinson, and John Dewey—leaders of the revolt against formalism, dogma, and tradition. Immensely excited at the potential of this liberation, Bourne became a skillful popularizer of Dewey's educational theories. As a member of the editorial staff of the *New Republic* after 1914, he participated prominently in the intellectuals' attack on nineteenth-century canons of taste and value in art, literature, and society. Indeed Professor Henry May styles Bourne "the nearly official voice of the Rebellion." In these prewar years Bourne's purpose, along with that of many young intellectuals, was to lead and goad his country into cultural and social maturity. He was optimistic about creating a new order, distinguished by reason and beauty, in the United States.

Initially Bourne's opposition to American participation in World War I ran counter to the sentiment of most American intellectuals. The doors of the magazines in which he published closed to him. But in June 1917, shortly before it was obliged to suspend operation (largely because of publishing his essays), *Seven Arts* accepted his scathing attack on the intellectuals' support of the war. The blood, Bourne declared, really lay on their hands. They had deliberately rationalized the war as a conflict "free from any taint of self-seeking," one that would "secure the triumph of democracy." Intellectuals had played a major role, according to Bourne, in overcoming the hesitation which other Americans experienced in regard to the war. For Bourne this was national tragedy. While Europe was fighting, Americans might have labored to clarify the meaning of democracy and to discover "a true Americanism." They might have concerned themselves with how democratic ends could be furthered throughout the world without resort to "the malevolent technique of war." But they "scarcely tried." As a result, Bourne continued, "the whole era has been spiritually wasted." Intellect was used "to lead an apathetic nation into an irresponsible war, without guarantees from those belligerents whose cause we were saving." In other words we went to war without any assurance that the new world order would be an improvement on the old. Bourne predicted that the league of nations some hoped would result from the war would be nothing more than "an armed truce." It would neither provide for legitimate national growth nor encourage economic internationalism but only petrify an order established by force.

Since Bourne regarded war as "the most noxious complex of all the evils that afflict men," it was with horror and disbelief that he saw his fellow intellectuals taking the lead in turning World War I into a holy crusade. For a disciple like Bourne the cruelest blow of all was to find John Dewey subscribing to the Wilsonian line. How, he wondered, could the foremost philosopher of American liberalism in his time be oblivious to the evil of war? Why were the pragmatists silent? If they answered that war was too strong a force to resist, Bourne countered: "how is it going to be weak enough for you to control and mould to your liberal purposes?" It seemed to him more likely that pragmatism concentrated so heavily on techniques and immediate consequences that it became incapable of either discovering or following long-term values and ideals. Dewey had said "not all who say *Ideals, Ideals,* shall enter the kingdom of the ideal, but only those shall enter who know and who respect the roads that conduct to the kingdom." But Bourne believed that this exclusive emphasis on means could result in the loss of ends altogether. The instrumentalist approach, for instance, focused on winning the war without considering whether the postwar world would be better or worse. As for democracy, it remained useful as a battle call or slogan but irrelevant to ultimate purposes. The problem with pragmatism in Bourne's eyes was that, while providing an effective way of determining the practical effects of ideals, it failed to explain how and why they were created. "We suffer," he concluded, "from a real shortage of spiritual values."

Admittedly one of those "who have taken Dewey's philosophy almost as our American religion," Bourne was deeply shaken by pragmatism's inability to meet the intellectual challenge of World War I. "One has a sense," he wrote in "Twilight of Idols" (1917), "of having come to a sudden, short stop at the end of an intellectual era." Taken in isolation such sentiment appears to suggest a lost generation interpretation of intellectuals and the war. Yet Bourne was less lost than he was disappointed and determined to restore vital, new idols to American thought. "The old ideals crumble; new ideals must be forged," he declared. Unhappy as he was with Dewey and most American intellectuals, he personally never lost the vision of his "private utopia" or the idealist's ability to go on "wild adventures" of the intellect. Pragmatism, at least in Dewey's hands, had failed the nation in time of crisis. All right, good riddance! True pragmatism, guided, Bourne hoped, by the memory of William James, would go on to better things. At his death in 1918 Bourne was experimenting with a vision of American society as a "world-federation in miniature" that would serve as a model for a world seeking a means of replacing belligerent nationalism with peaceful pluralism. In such thinking Bourne rode the mainstream of American mission.

Professor Carl Resek has pointed out that the legend of Bourne as an embittered and cynical outcast—the first member of the lost generation—has been difficult to transcend. Indeed Bourne's physical deformity, linking him to characters wounded in the war such as

Jake Barnes in Hemingway's *The Sun Also Rises,* seemed to symbolize his frustration and despair. Resek mentions a dozen memoirs as well as several poems and novels that repeat the Bourne myth. Yet the real Bourne never lost his desire for progress or his faith that America, if it resisted false prophets, could remain a messiah. Likewise Bourne had no quarrel with the American past. In his autobiographical "The History of a Literary Radical," published posthumously in 1919, he expressed confidence that the best of tradition and the iconoclasm of the war generation could be fused into cultural distinction. Indeed Bourne was more rebellious, nihilistic, and discontented while leading the prewar cultural rebellion as a Greenwich Village radical than he was in 1917 and 1918. Far from causing him to reject values and ideals, the war brought him a renewed conviction of their importance. There is every indication that, had he lived, Bourne would not have been one of the allegedly lost intellectuals of the 1920s with which he is so frequently associated. For Bourne "standing at the end of an era," as he expressed it, implied an urgency to create, not a reason to resign.

Randolph Bourne died before the peace negotiations at Versailles and the American response to the League of Nations had been played to their unhappy conclusions, but he expected as much. For those intellectuals who supported the war effort, however, there was surprise and guilt. The *New Republic,* the unofficial voice of the liberal intellectuals in this period, reacted in typical fashion. At the time of the Armistice in November 1918 its editors basked in the belief that "at this instant in history, democracy is supreme." But less than a year later they published an article by John Dewey that can be read only as an apologia for his earlier position in regard to the war. Entitled "The Discrediting of Idealism," it expressed Dewey's agonized recognition that the war had brought no new day in international affairs, no triumph of democracy, and no guarantee of peace. Although self-consciously avoiding use of the first person, Dewey virtually acknowledged that he had been among "the gullible throng who swallowed the cant of idealism as a sugar coating for the bitter core of violence and greed." Naive optimism and "fine phrases," according to Dewey, led Americans to the assumption that ideals would be served merely by victory, while blinding them to such realities as the secret treaties among the other Allies. He had the grace, however, not to blame President Wilson for the debacle. Ultimate blame, Dewey concluded, must lie with Americans, and particularly with its intellectuals, for not distinguishing between intelligent and futile use of force.

It is important to realize that John Dewey, like Randolph Bourne, did not abandon himself to cynicism and despair after becoming disillusioned with World War I. Indeed the final pages of "The Discrediting of Idealism" were directed to the problem of reviving idealism, by associating it with nonmilitary forces such as commerce, industry, and science. And, of course, Dewey went on in the 1920s with his career as a creative and multifaceted philosopher, following many of the same trails he had pioneered before 1917. He emerged from the war experience sobered, sadder but wiser, yet not at all in accord with the usual image of the intellectual of the lost generation.

These examples point to the need for a more precise statement of the relationship between the war and the American intellectual. In the first place there was disillusion with the war, but it was *with the war*—not necessarily, or even logically, with the whole of American thought, culture, and tradition. Too often this distinction has been blurred by historians anxious to use World War I to explain the alleged alienation of intellectuals in the 1920s.

Actual disillusion took several forms. Unquestionably American intellectuals were revolted by war as a solution to man's problems. The absurdity of using a war to end all wars, of instituting freedom with force, quickly became apparent after 1918. Dewey's essay the following year was only the first in a long line of condemnations of America's intervention in the European conflict. Revisionist histories such as Harry Elmer Barnes' *Genesis of the World War* (1926) have picked apart the various threads in the fabric of war causation and concluded that Germany was not solely responsible. In 1928 Sidney B. Fay's *Origins of the World War* argued convincingly that Allied propaganda had distorted the facts. The conclusion that most thoughtful Americans reached during the 1920s was that the war had been a horrible mistake.

Another target of disillusion was internationalism. Americans, led by the intellectuals, had put their altruism on the line in 1917 and failed dismally to improve the condition of the world. Bitterness and hurt pride resulted. Intellectuals joined the people in vowing never again to commit their ideals and energies to foreign causes. The rejection of the Treaty of Versailles, including the League of

Nations, was only the most obvious example of this mentality in action. While isolationism has been discredited as an accurate description of United States foreign policy following World War I, there is no doubt that an emotional turning-inward was pervasive. It is evident in classic form in the statement of the drama critic George Jean Nathan: "the great problems of the world—social, political, economic and theological—do not concern me in the slightest. If all the Armenians were to be killed tomorrow and if half of Russia were to starve to death the day after, it would not matter to me in the least. What concerns me alone is myself, and the interests of a few close friends. For all I care the rest of the world may go to hell at today's sunset." Such had not been the attitude of previous generations of American intellectuals who, in fact, had been very much concerned with the starving Armenians and other unfortunates abroad. But the war temporarily eclipsed the liberal creed as it concerned foreigners. The new orientation, as Nathan implied, was toward one's own navel.

World War I also produced a sense of concern verging on fear for the future of the Western world. The spectacle of what were assumed to be the world's most civilized nations attempting to cut each others' throats dealt the assumption of uninterrupted progress a rude jolt. What had become of reason, of ethics, indeed of the will to survive? Was Western civilization descending into middle age? A book that both reflected and encouraged this frame of mind appeared in Germany in 1918: Oswald Spengler's *The Decline of the West*. His point was that Western civilization was doomed by the rhythm of cultures to decline and perish just as had ancient Greece and Rome. Although an American edition appeared in 1926, *The Decline of the West* did not become a best-seller in the United States. Most professional historians deprecated Spengler's thesis, as they later did that of Arnold Toynbee. But especially in the larger community of educated people Spengler raised nagging doubts. The world war made it impossible to ignore the possibility that civilization in the West might be on the verge of a breakdown. In the United States, moreover, the end of three centuries of frontier provided an additional reason for uneasiness. From some points of view the advent of an urban-industrial civilization and the loss of pioneer vitality meant decline rather than progress.

In some ways Henry Adams was the American counterpart of Oswald Spengler. *The Education of Henry Adams* was written a decade before World War I but by some stroke of luck or genius its publication was withheld until 1918 when the postwar mood helped make it the best-selling work of nonfiction in 1919 and the recipient of the Pulitzer Prize for autobiography the following year. Like Spengler, Adams expressed the belief that the modern world might be accelerating toward destruction rather than perfection. Adams too looked back to the ancient, dead civilizations for analogies and wrote ominously of forces far outstripping man's ability to control them. He even made so bold as to suggest that evolution might bring retrogression.

Although Adams reached his conclusions in *The Education* without the assistance of World War I, the degree of his pessimism was extreme even for the postwar American mind. Yet the popularity of the book suggests that the war had heightened the awareness of a good many American intellectuals that the prewar belief in progress stood on shallow foundations. Undoubtedly Freudian theory with its idea of the death wish and its primitivistic assumption of the unhappiness of civilized men also contributed to the apprehension. Confidence in the future, at any rate, had experienced considerable erosion since the time when Americans had stood with Theodore Roosevelt at Armageddon and battled for the Lord. But this was no reason for intellectuals to deprecate the past or surrender to nihilism. What this nervous generation needed *most* was tradition and value. In regard to the war, disillusion had its limits.

The attitudes of American intellectuals toward the war were clearly illustrated in the immediate postwar years. There was the initial, intense disappointment, expressed, for instance, in the innumerable and widely read war books. In many cases disillusion led to physical separation from the United States—to expatriation, as it was called. But even in the cafes of Paris the intellectuals could not forget their homeland. In spirit they were still Americans. Thus the term "expatriation" really overstates the point. Better is Malcolm Cowley's "exile." And Cowley, who personally fled to Europe, was astute in sensing the homesick attitude of the exiles, their hunger for childhood certainties. "It was not by accident," Cowley wrote in *Exile's Return*, "that their early books were almost all nostalgic, full of the wish to recapture some remembered thing. In Paris or Pamplona, writing, drinking, watching bullfights or making love, they continued to desire a Kentucky hill cabin, a farmhouse in Iowa or Wisconsin, the Michigan woods, the blue Juniata, a country they had 'lost, ah, lost,' as Thomas Wolfe kept saying; a home to which they couldn't go back." Yet, in the end, Cowley described how the exiles did go back to an America which, it is implied, they never really left.

It is possible to detect in the enthusiasm of some American liberals for the Russian Revolution of 1917 the attitude of men envying a country that had not gone wrong. Of course only a few actually joined the Harvard radical John Reed on the battlements, but for a time after 1917 many American intellectuals transferred their hopes for the common man to the red flag. Only later in the 1920s, as the regime of Lenin gave way to that of Stalin, did they come to see that Russia, too, had problems.

Even while disappointed with their country, the attitude of American intellectuals was one of relief that the weaknesses of the old order were finally exposed. Now, perhaps, reconstruction of a better America could begin. The war had been a needed catharsis. In such a spirit Harold Stearns edited *Civilization in the United States* (1922), a volume that has strangely become known as a leading example of the intellectuals' alienation from their country and a portrayal of America as a wasteland. It is true that the book's many contributors painted a grey picture of the state of the national culture and that editor Stearns left for Paris immediately upon completing his labors. But the book's prevailing mood was one of hope and encouragement, not hatred and despair. Stearns struck this tone in his preface, declaring the book to be harsh but "constructive criticism," an effort to clear the rocks in order to make the sowing of "a real civilization" possible. Stearns went on to score the emotional and aesthetic sterility of his society; he pointed out that "we have no heritages or traditions to which to cling except those that have already withered in our hands and turned to dust." Yet he was drawn back to the thought that America had "rich" as well as "disastrous" potentialities. And, changing his mind about withered heritages, he called upon his countrymen "to appraise and warmly to cherish the heterogeneous elements which make up our life." Reacceptance now accomplished, Stearns mused: "It is curious how a book on American civilization actually leads one back to the conviction that we are, after all, Americans."

Stearns' own chapter in *Civilization in the United States* on "The Intellectual Life" was an amplification of this ambivalence. He began with the idea that America's pioneering past, its utilitarian orientation, stamped a contempt for intellectual values on the national character. In fact, Stearns admitted, he was tempted to subtitle his essay "A Study in Sterility." He did not, however, because he did not believe it. "Beneath the surface barrenness stirs a germinal energy that may yet push its way through the weeds and the tin-cans of those who are afraid of life." According to Stearns, hope lay in the rebelliousness of the young intellectuals. The war had opened their eyes, shown them the sandy foundations of the older generation's beliefs. But they were not prepared to reject America and its entire past. They found value in writers such as Walt Whitman, Mark Twain, and Henry David Thoreau. Intellectuals of the twenties, Stearns continued, believed it possible to sublimate the "vitality and nervous alertness" of American life into cultural greatness. They were crusaders, not cynics.

At the conclusion of his essay Stearns launched a remarkable paean, completely contrary to his reputation in American intellectual history:

Climb to the top of the Palisades and watch the great city [New York] in the deepening dusk as light after light, and rows of lights after rows, topped by towers of radiance at the end of the island, shine through the shadows across the river. Think, then, of the miles of rolling plains, fertile and dotted with cities, stretching behind one to that other ocean . . . , of the millions of human aspirations and hopes and youthful eagernesses contained in the great sprawling, uneasy entity we call our country—must all the hidden beauty and magic and laughter we know is ours be quenched because we lack the courage to make it proud and defiant? Or walk down the Avenue [Fifth, in New York City] some late October morning when the sun sparkles in a clear and electric air such as can be found nowhere else in the world. The flashing beauty of form, the rising step of confident animalism, the quick smile of fertile minds—must all these things, too, be reduced to a drab uniformity because we lack the courage to proclaim their sheer physical loveliness? Has not the magic of America been hidden under a fog of ugliness by those who never really loved it, who never knew our natural gaiety and high spirits and eagerness for knowledge? They have the upper hand now—but who would dare to prophesy that they can keep it?

Stearns' passionate, almost mystical, tribute has been ignored by historians of the 1920s because, one suspects, it does not fit the stereotyped understanding of intellectuals in the period. Yet it stands prominently in a book widely taken to be a manifesto of disgust with and alienation from the United States. Clearly Stearns' reputation is in need of reassessment. A man so basically in love with his country is hardly a fitting representative of the lost generation.

The problem, of course, is that this stereotype is distorted. Disillusion certainly existed among intellectuals in the twenties, but with neither the indiscriminate coverage nor the intensity that most observers have supposed. It is clear that Stearns regarded his generation of young intellectuals as *better* lovers of the nation than the Puritans and the philistines. His final question, above, revealed that he was not pessimistic about bringing off a cultural revolution. The shackles of utilitarianism and gentility could be broken, if not in the United States, then, for the time being, by Americans in Paris. But the goal remained an American intellectual renaissance.

Man

On June 1, 1924, breakfasting Americans opened their morning newspapers and bent curiously over the front page headlines: fourteen-year-old Bobby Franks had been brutally murdered in Chicago. Murders, to be sure, were nothing new to the 1920s and especially not to Al Capone's Chicago, but the papers labeled this one "the crime of the century." Details followed. On May 21 Nathan F. Leopold, Jr., aged nineteen, and Richard A. Loeb, eighteen, rented a car and drove past a private school. Leopold and Loeb had not selected a victim, but when Bobby Franks came into sight they stopped their car beside him. Loeb, who knew the boy slightly, persuaded him to accept a ride home. Shortly before reaching that destination, however, Bobby was struck over the head with a taped, steel chisel and pulled onto the floor of the back seat. When he continued to make noises he was gagged and smothered in a lap robe. In a few moments he was dead. The murderers wrapped the corpse in the robe and waited for darkness. They then drove to an isolated spot in the South Chicago marshes, undressed their victim, and poured hydrochloric acid over his face and body. What remained was stuffed into a culvert under the Pennsylvania Railroad tracks. For several days the reason for Bobby's disappearance eluded police and his frantic parents. Finally a pair of eyeglasses, dropped near the culvert, led to the arrest of Leopold and the exposure of the murder about which Americans read on June 1.

What made the murder of Bobby Franks one of the most publicized crimes in American history was the character of the murderers. Neither Leopold nor Loeb was the type of person the public expected to be a criminal. Both were sons of well-to-do lawyers, raised with every advantage. Moreover, both were highly intelligent. Nathan Leopold had been a precocious baby, walking and talking before he was six months old. Subsequent intelligence tests revealed an exceptional mind—Leopold scored in the genius category, between 200 and 210 points. He entered the University of Chicago at fourteen and, four years later, became the youngest graduate in that institution's history. Two days after murdering Bobby Franks, Leopold casually passed the entrance examinations for the Harvard Law School with superior scores. Richard Loeb was also brilliant, a college graduate at eighteen, and a student in graduate school at the time of the crime.

From every rational consideration the kidnapping and murder of Bobby Franks were pointless. In the cases of Leopold and Loeb the crime could not be blamed on need or on environment or on lack of intelligence. The murderers seemed to have the best, not the worst, of such things. In addition, Leopold and Loeb had no grudge against Bobby Franks or his family; the choice of their victim had been entirely random. Their crime, in short, could not be explained rationally. Yet it certainly occurred, as Leopold and Loeb smilingly admitted when confronted with the evidence.

The inconsistency between Leopold and Loeb's actions and the behavior traditionally expected of people in their circumstances alerted Americans of 1924 to the possibility that their accustomed understanding of human nature was in need of radical revision. Could it be that men did not act entirely, or perhaps even largely, from reasoned judgment? Were intelligence, education, and background no guarantee of socially acceptable behavior? Was not man basically good?

While behavior such as that of Leopold and Loeb negated the accustomed assumptions of American social thought, a new concept of human nature which had been emerging since the 1890s was fully prepared to explain such phenomena. Its architects were psychologists, scientists of the mind, and the impact of their ideas on American intellectual history in the 1920s was profound. Not only criminals but, it seemed, everyone was susceptible to motivation by other than rational or moral forces.

In Europe the discussion of the mind in other than religious or romantic terms was already well advanced when William James published *Principles of Psychology* in 1890.

Building on the insights of Charles Darwin, James presented a naturalistic and functionalistic interpretation of mental processes. Instead of a controlling influence guiding men to ethical behavior and linking them to God, James contended that the mind was merely a physical organ. It had evolved like a leg or an eye and had no supernatural properties. The mind functioned as a tool enabling man to adjust to his environment. For most American intellectuals this entirely biological conception of human nature dealt a mortal blow to the old dualistic view of the mind as distinct from the physical body. After the functionalists, for example, there seemed no basis for following Transcendentalism in its assumption that each man contained a soul—a "spark of divinity"—which inclined him toward the good.

Shortly before World War I psychology began to have considerable impact on the way American intellectuals conceived of human nature. Some spoke of ancient, inherited instincts as the determinants of behavior; others pointed to the endocrine glands as the sources of conduct. Those who rejected this reliance on heredity and physiology in favor of a strictly environmental explanation of thought and action, the behaviorists, took their inspiration and name from a 1914 book by John B. Watson, *Behavior: An Introduction to Comparative Psychology.* Its argument rested on the idea of stimulus-response. The Russian psychologist Ivan Pavlov's experiments with dogs and other animals had alerted Watson to parallels in the human situation. He went on to develop the image of the hollow man. According to this view, men lacked the capacity for self-direction. They responded only to external stimuli as a dog, at the sound of a bell, salivated in expectation of food. Of course responses could be conditioned by training, but there was no place for choice in this mechanistic conception of the mind. Watson continued publishing into the twenties, his *Behaviorism* (1925) receiving special acclaim.

Even as behaviorism flourished, another school of psychology was gaining such popularity that it would in time relegate the behaviorists to minor status. Indeed the impact of Sigmund Freud on American intellectual history of the 1920s might be compared to that of Darwin in the late nineteenth century or Locke in Revolutionary times. Unlike the behaviorists, the Austrian-born genius and his followers did not consider minds hollow. On the contrary, the Freudians posited an elaborate mental structure seething with conscious and unconscious currents. To use the familiar "iceberg" metaphor, Freud argued that only a small part of the mind was "out of the water" in the realm of consciousness and rationality. This part he labeled the *ego*. Below the water level of consciousness, and much larger, as is the case with icebergs, was the *id*. Freud used this term to denote the totality of drives, passions, and impulses. The core of his theory was that these dark, irrational depths strongly influenced thought and behavior. At the very bottom of the id Freud located the *libido*, the province of sexuality.

Freudian psychology posited an eternal conflict between the ego and the id over the direction of the individual. With the aid of ideals and ethics (the *superego*), reason attempted to control the destructive energy of the unconscious. But, as the iceberg analogy suggests, size and strength were on the id's side. The ego, consequently, resorted to trickery. It attempted by means of *sublimation* to channel the dark power of the id into higher and more beneficial forms of expression. Its partial success was the only way Freud could explain responsibility and social existence. Yet Freud also recognized that too much repression of the urges of the unconscious produced mental sicknesses—*neuroses*. His task as a psychoanalyst was to help the ego discipline the id and still permit expression of hidden desires and anxieties. Nothing in Freudian theory fascinated Americans of the 1920s more than this idea of repression and release.

The American understanding of and interest in Freud may be given practical illustration by reference to the Leopold and Loeb case. The initial public reaction was to demand retribution—quick death to the murderers. At the trial late in the summer of 1924 the prosecution echoed these sentiments, branding the accused cold-blooded fiends. But the famous trial lawyer Clarence Darrow, who undertook the defense of Leopold and Loeb despite their plea of guilty, gradually engineered a remarkable change in attitude. Using the testimony of prominent psychiatrists and emphasizing that the murder was totally lacking in ordinary motives, Darrow succeeded in shifting the focus of the trial to the condition of the murderers' minds. His point was that, in spite of their great intelligence, Leopold and Loeb were driven by forces beyond their control to perform senseless acts of aggression and destruction. Drawing straight from Freud, Darrow argued in his plea to the court that "brains are not the chief essential in human conduct." It was, rather, the unconscious impulses (Darrow called them "emotions") that determined action. Normally, Darrow continued, the ethical and moral habits instilled in children at an early age sufficed to check the beast beneath. In Darrow's words, "these habits are supposed to be strong enough so that they will form inhibitions against conduct when the emotions come in conflict with the duties of life." But the minds of Leopold and Loeb were "diseased"; they could not suppress the dark, senseless urges that resulted in the murder of Bobby Franks. Moreover, Darrow implied, we all had such unconscious drives and differed only in our ability to control them. Instead of screaming for the blood of the accused, we should walk humbly in the knowledge that we too are capable of antisocial acts.

Darrow's purpose in taking the Leopold and Loeb case was not to exonerate them but only to save their lives from what he regarded an antiquated system of jurisprudence. In this he succeeded. His plea convinced the court that Leopold and Loeb were victims of insanity rather than practitioners of criminality. Their sentence, it followed, was life imprisonment rather than death.

The vogue of Freudian psychology in the United States began in 1909 when the master himself came to lecture at Clark University at the invitation of its president, the eminent educational psychologist G. Stanley Hall. Shortly thereafter A. A. Brill, a New York physician who had studied under Freud in Vienna, began to translate and publicize Freud's writings for the American audience. Initially the merits of Freudianism were hotly debated both in the intellectual community and at the popular level. Walter Lippmann, for one, accepted the new view of man and, as early as 1912, began to think about its implications for politics (see page 57). Others refused to relinquish a belief in man's goodness and rationality. It was especially painful for American intellectuals to admit that intelligence counted for as little as Freud supposed. The chief popular opposition to Freud came from those who understood his ideas to be a rationale for lust and sin.

With World War I, however, came telling new evidence for the psychologists' view of human nature. The British and French deluged Americans with atrocity propaganda. Its purpose was to convince them, the facts notwithstanding, that everything right and good was on the Allied side while the Huns were sadistic and lecherous beasts. One widely circulated poster depicted in silhouette a huge, armed German dragging a young girl by the hair. The written reports were more explicit still. As this propaganda poured into the United States in 1915 and 1916, it probably occurred to few that it rested on a conception of man posited by the psychologists. Yet here was a subtle campaign to reach the recesses of the mind. Truth was clearly subordinated to the attainment of ends—in this case American support of the Allies.

After April 1917 the United States government launched its own propaganda operation. Psychology was dressed in uniform and made to serve the cause. Over a hundred psychologists, many of them distinguished professors, volunteered their services in the task of picking recruits. Intelligence tests, including Professor Lewis Terman's much discussed Intelligence Quotient (I.Q.) scale, were applied to thousands of potential soldiers. Woodrow Wilson appointed a Committee on Public Information, headed by George Creel, which was instructed to win support for the American war effort. Creel and his associates, including many intellectuals, believed they could make men think the way the war leaders desired. The hollow men (following the behaviorists) could be filled with the proper ideas through the use of the correct stimuli. Or the unconscious (following the Freudians) could be tapped in the interest of directing public opinion. Creel personally conceived of his job as "the fight for the minds of men, for the 'conquest of their convictions.' "

The Committee on Public Information carried this fight into every American community and practically into every home. Scholars contributed to *Red, White and Blue* pamphlets deprecating the "blond beast" and allegedly illustrating how German ideals were antipodal to those Americans held. A corps of speakers known as the Four Minute Men delivered over seven million four-minute speeches during intermissions of movies and other public functions.

Some of the techniques Creel used were primitive. Sauerkraut, a German dish, was officially renamed liberty cabbage; hamburger became liberty sandwich. Squads of patriots ranged the countryside pressing the sale of war bonds. Men suspected of disloyalty were made to kiss the flag. Germans and those who opposed the war were hounded without mercy. The end effect was to create an atmosphere in which reason and free choice counted for little.

And it worked! The Creel committee succeeded in goading most Americans including intellectuals into a frenzy of loyalty. Only later did some pause to consider that they had been manipulated by emotional symbols and stereotyped characterizations. It no longer appeared necessary to appeal to reasoned argument to sway men's belief. The psychologists, it seemed, were correct in their estimate of the mind.

After its completion George Creel wrote a book about the work of the Committee on Public Information entitled *How We Advertised America*, and it did not take enterprising American businessmen long to discern the peacetime potential of high pressure advertising. As books like *The Psychology of Package Labels* and *The Psychology of Selling Life Insurance* made clear, demand for a particular product could be created irrespective of its merits merely by associating it with emotion-laden symbols and appealing to deeply rooted human urges. Psychology became the key to the great age of advertising which World War I ushered into American life.

Edward L. Bernays illustrates the connection between Freud, war, and advertising. Bernays was a nephew of Sigmund Freud who as a young man adopted New York City as his home. During World War I he served on the Creel committee, gaining experience in the techniques of creating and controlling opinion. After the war Bernays carried his knowledge into the world of business. He became the prototype public relations counselor. In the manner of Freud, Bernays believed that prejudices with roots running far down into the unconscious determined human thought and conduct. Rather than attempt to change these basic impulses, he urged businessmen to relate their products to them in such a way that people would make a purchase. The sex drive, for instance, made it desirable to associate a product in a newspaper or magazine advertisement with a picture of an attractive young lady. The lack of logical relation between curves and cars or cigarettes made little difference to the advertising theorists for whom sales were the ultimate criterion.

Understandably the nascent advertising firms eagerly sought the services of professional psychologists. In 1924, for example, John B. Watson, the pioneering behaviorist, became vice president of the nation's leading advertising agency. A professor of psychology at Columbia University, Albert T. Poffenberger, wrote *Psychology in Advertising* in 1925 and immediately was in demand as a consultant. Poffenberger's lengthy book showed in word and illustration how clever advertisements could take advantage of unconscious elements in the mind. Color, shape, and arrangement had great significance. Toward the end of his book, Poffenberger turned from specifics to theory. "Belief," he declared, "is a matter of feeling and emotion rather than reason. The truth is not a primary factor in determining belief." Until the advent of psychology, Americans had accepted the opposite as a matter of course. The new emphasis on social control through applied psychology was also apparent in books with revealing titles: *Man the Puppet: The Art of Controlling Minds* (1925) by Abram Lipsky, *Means of Social Control* (1925) by Frederick E. Lumley, and *Influencing Human Behavior* (also 1925) by H. A. Overstreet.

The impact of the *new psychology* extended far beyond American advertising. Originally an esoteric branch of medical knowledge, psychology was broadened and diluted in the 1920s to become a popular fad. Oversimplification and sensationalism followed, especially with reference to the ideas of Sigmund Freud. Dozens of condensed "summaries" of Freudian theory appeared, as did books ranging from *The Psychology of Jesus* to *The Psychology of Golf*, and prepared do-it-yourself psychoanalytic aids such as *Ten Thousand Dreams Interpreted*. Since very few Americans read Freud in the original (a comparison with the equally unread Darwin is pertinent), such popularizations were of the utmost importance in disseminating ideas. Often much of the qualification and even the import of the message were lost in the translation of the idea from creator to public. American conversation became salted with words like "complex," "neurosis," "fixation," and "Freudian slip." The *New York Times* carried a serious article explaining the popular song *Yes, We Have No Bananas* in terms of a national inferiority complex.

The unfortunate result was that on the broadest level to which Freudian psychology filtered its meaning was something akin to a justification of having fun. More responsible custodians of Freudianism among the intellectuals endeavored to integrate the full implications of psychology into their particular disciplines. Often this was not easy since the antiintellectual implications of Freudian theory were unmistakable. James Harvey Robinson, an historian and a leader of the revolt against formalism in the social sciences, came away from a study of Freud with the conviction that irrational forces exercised the dominant influence on man's thought and conduct. There was no such thing as pure reason. What we called reason was really only rationalization for actions that our animal impulses commanded us to do. "The result," Robinson contended, "is that most of our so-called reasoning consists in finding arguments for going on believing as we already do." This not only relegated reason to an inferior position but destroyed its separate identity altogether. John Dewey likewise placed the intellect in a subordinate position. His *Human Nature and Conduct* (1922) argued for the primacy of innate "instincts" and irrational "habits" in determining behavior. Throughout the book Dewey demonstrated a talent for using Freudian concepts such as fantasy, repression, and sublimation. He proved equally adept with the stimulus-response concepts of the behaviorists. From either viewpoint intelligence seemed a weak reed.

American letters quickly responded to the new understanding of human nature. In the writing of history and biography it became commonplace after World War I to investigate the parental relationships, sex life, and dreams of one's subject with the object of explaining his behavior in psychoanalytic terms. Harold D. Lasswell's *Psychopathology and Politics* (1930) was representative in the way it put past political figures "on the couch." The principal effect of such scholarship was to lower the reader's estimation of the person discussed. In fact the word "debunking" was coined in the twenties to characterize the new style. The overall results, however, seldom equaled expectations, in large part because of the scarcity of data on which the psychoanalysis of historical figures could be based.

Writers of fiction and drama with an esthetic, as opposed to a scholarly, purpose, used Freud to better advantage. The findings of the psychologists gave the novelists rich new veins to mine in discussing motivation and human relations. Theodore Dreiser's early novels, such as *Sister Carrie* (1900), treated men and women as helpless pawns in the hands of powerful natural forces. At this time Dreiser's naturalism stemmed largely from Darwin and his purpose was to show that man was subject to an animal's compulsive urges.

In the next quarter century Freudianism came to be a major intellectual force in the United States. When Dreiser published *An American Tragedy* in 1925 he added the mind to the forces driving man against his will and often against his best interests. The protagonist of this novel, Clyde Griffiths, is a prisoner of a sensuality which ultimately proves his undoing.

Sex, of course, was the chief component of Freud's unconscious, and the psychological school of writers saturated their work with it. Sherwood Anderson's *Many Marriages* (1923) explores a man who rejects a frigid wife in order to release his sexual drives and, it is implied, lives a full life with his secretary. *Dark Laughter* (1925) focuses on the contrast between the allegedly neurotic white community and the unrepressed, primitivistic black one. "If there is anything you do not understand in human life," one of its characters remarks, "consult the works of Dr. Freud." Intellectuals, Anderson made clear, were particularly incapable of releasing their desires and hence particularly unhappy. Anderson's best-known work, *Winesburg, Ohio* (1919) describes in almost clinical fashion the twisted minds and lives of the citizens of a small town.

To a greater or lesser extent Freud's mark was visible on most fiction of the 1920s. In some cases the influence was clear and acknowledged. "I'm hipped on Freud and all that," an F. Scott Fitzgerald heroine remarks, "but its rotten that every bit of *real* love in the world is ninety-nine percent passion and one little soupçon of jealousy." "Don't you even know, mother," a flapper in John Howard Lawson's *Loudspeaker* declares, "that everybody's thoughts are obscenely vile? That's psychology." Other authors' use of the science of the mind could be detected only in their references to a darker presence behind the civilized exterior. Thus Percy Marks' *The Plastic Age* (1924) describes a college dance as going "on and on, the constant rhythmic wailing of the fiddles, syncopated passion screaming with lust, the drums, horribly primitive; drunken embraces."

In American theater of the 1920s the preeminent Freudian was Eugene O'Neill. The playwright also drew heavily on the ideas of Carl Jung, a onetime disciple of Freud who broke with the master over the nature of the motivating forces in the unconscious. Jung's theory that every individual possesses a memory of the history of his race (the racial unconscious) is the crux of *The Emperor Jones* (1920). In this play a black Pullman porter rises to be dictator over a primitive tribe only to succumb to terrifying hallucinations of his race's African and slave past. A similar inability to escape the racial unconscious brings a white girl to hate the black law student she has married in *All God's Chillun Got Wings* (1924). O'Neill experimented imaginatively with the dramatic portrayal of schizophrenia, sadism, incest, the Oedipus complex, and other irrational behavior. His greatest success in this line was *Strange Interlude* (1928), an exploration of the reactions of a girl denied union with her lover by a disapproving father.

The American idea of human nature underwent a striking transformation between 1910 and 1925. Psychology provided the theoretical framework for the new view, while dramatic incidents, like the Leopold and Loeb murder, furnished concrete evidence. Not everyone, of course, rushed to embrace the revised estimation of man. The older view was certainly more flattering and, for the bulk of the people, probably the only one they knew. But among the intellectuals the percentage of acceptance was far higher. The new ideas, especially the Freudian concept of repression, made perfect ammunition for the intellectuals in the twenties in their attacks on both puritanism and gentility. The philosophical primitivism implicit in much of Freudianism provided support for the widespread feeling that modern men suffered from the malaise of overcivilization. American intellectuals also welcomed Freud because he offered a way of interpreting, if not ameliorating, the senseless, destructive behavior that had seemed so large a part of life since 1914. Be it war, murder, suicide, or merely flagpole sitting, the Freudians at least had an explanation and some claim to being scientific.

Democracy

As it took shape in the eighteenth and nineteenth centuries, democratic political theory rested on the assumption that man was a rational being, capable of directing his affairs for the greatest good. On these grounds the public could be trusted with political power. The voice of the people, early democrats frequently said, most closely approximated the voice of God. Calvinistic pessimism and the idea of original sin were unfounded. Thomas Jefferson, for one, argued that education alone was necessary to assure the success of democracy. Although John Adams and his fellow Federalists had less faith in unguided man, they still believed that government could be designed along republican principles so that the people could safely exercise sovereignty. Emerson and other romantics put less emphasis on reason, but they invested every man with a capacity for intuiting and following the right. Indeed the main tenet of American liberalism before the twentieth century held that only an imperfect environment stood between a basically good humanity and perfection. Democracy thrived on this faith in the average man's goodness and capability.

For the most part early American intellectuals championed the democratic ideal. But by the 1920s sufficient doubts about democracy had entered American thought to cause considerable uncertainty. For one thing, the frontier conditions that many had linked to democracy's rise and success in the New World were unquestionably vanishing. Second, the size and complexity of twentieth-century American civilization seemed to have outstripped the governing ability of the general public. But, most importantly, psychology undermined democracy. James, Watson, and Freud postulated a conception of human nature that differed radically from that held by the early republicans. After the psychologists had spoken, man could no longer be confidently regarded as master of his fate. Instead he seemed driven by forces that he neither fully understood nor controlled. It seemed impossible to reconcile the behavior of Leopold and Loeb, for instance, with Jefferson's faith in the beneficence of an educated, intelligent electorate. And the mounting evidence that opinion could be molded to any purpose by propaganda and advertising made it difficult to sustain the notion of free, responsible political action. If Freud was right about the relative strengths of reason and the unconscious, then democracy's foundation lay in sand.

These possibilities triggered a major debate among American intellectuals during World War I and on into the following decade. Some concluded that republicanism was a naive dream. But the greater number were reluctant to abandon that faith in the individual and in self-government which had been the core of American liberalism for so long. Salvage, adaptation, and reconstruction resulted. Democracy was retooled to fit twentieth-century assumptions and realities. Final adjustments, to be sure, awaited the 1930s and, for that matter, continue today, but in the twenties American minds first came to grips with the problem of democracy in modern civilization.

Walter Lippmann had been among the first American intellectuals to absorb the significance of Freudianism, and he led the way in drawing its conclusions for democracy. As early as 1914 Lippmann's *A Preface to Politics* argued that democracy ignored the realities of human nature that the psychologists were discovering. "The impetus of Freud," he declared, "is perhaps the greatest advance ever made towards the understanding and control of human character." Psychology, however, was not yet sufficiently refined to accept the challenge of the complexity of politics. "It will take time and endless labor for a detailed study of social problems in the light of this growing knowledge" of the mind, he warned.

By 1922 Lippmann was more confident. The war had exposed human nature more clearly while continued refinements in the science of the mind promised better interpretations of the new evidence. And in 1922 Lippmann published *Public Opinion,* a book of rare insight and courage which fulfilled his earlier call for a psychology of politics.

In *Public Opinion* Lippmann endeavored to draw the connection between the way people thought and the assumptions of democratic theory. His point, in essence, was that democracy could not work because public opinion was irrational. Lippmann began his argument with the basic premise of philosophical idealism—to be is to be perceived. In other words, the "pictures in our heads" did not necessarily, or even frequently, correspond to "the world outside." In fact most of what we knew about our environment was a highly subjective mélange of prejudice, moral judgment, and *stereotypes*—a word Lippmann borrowed from the printing trade and made famous in this book. Stereotypes, according to Lippmann, were distorted preconceptions that people held about various parts of the external world. Such giant generalizations became increasingly essential as the environment became too large and complex for the individual to assimilate. Thus it was easier, for instance, to stereotype all socialists as bearded, bomb-tossing anarchists than to consider each radical as a distinct person. Similarly most persons lumped Jews, Negroes, and other minorities into one convenient image. Stereotypes, Lippmann contended, did not result from an objective consideration of the facts. They were warped and irrational characterizations in which the Freudian subconscious figured as the major determinant. Yet on such shaky bases, Lippmann believed, people made decisions.

World War I provided Walter Lippmann with a case study in

the formation of public opinion. He observed how first the British and then the American government had succeeded in cultivating stereotypes of the Germans on the one hand and the Allies on the other. Capitalizing on the public's inability to challenge the selected facts and outright lies it received, the propagandists deliberately manipulated men's minds into a warlike frame. To a less dramatic extent the same process occurred in peacetime. Politicians, pressure groups, advertisers, and the dispensers of "news" (which Lippmann carefully distinguished from "truth") artfully fashioned the stereotypes with which the average man ordered his existence. Equally potent as opinion-makers were parents, teachers, clergy, and vocational superiors.

The implications of public opinion formation for democracy frightened Lippmann. Traditional democratic theory assumed that individuals could assimilate facts, reason, judge for themselves, and arrive at the closest possible approximation of truth. But in the light of twentieth-century experience such assumptions did not appear justified. The problem was that democratic theory had been developed at a time when political communities were small and self-contained. Opinion could arise spontaneously from a full set of facts readily at hand, and the public could act competently on this basis. In these town meeting circumstances democracy worked. But the resemblance of such conditions to the United States of 1922 was slight. Political problems had become so large and so diverse that the individual voter had little chance of even knowing them all, much less of attaining the expertise necessary to reach effective solutions.

Other intellectuals joined Lippmann in criticizing democracy. Ralph Adams Cram, an eminent architect of the 1920s with an admiration for the medieval style in society as well as in buildings, scorned representative government and universal suffrage as leading only to mediocrity. Quality had been forgotten in the emphasis on quantity, on majority rule. Writing in 1917 in *The Nemesis of Mediocrity* Cram alleged that democratic methods had "reduced all mankind to the dead level of incapacity." Great leaders are lacking, "while society itself is unable, of its own power as a whole, to lift itself from the nadir of its own uniformity." In Cram's opinion "the great mass of men have always been of the Neolithic type"; hence to trust them with their own government is the sheerest of idiocy. " 'The world must be made safe for democracy' is a noble phrase," he concluded, "but it is meaningless without its corollary, 'democracy must be made safe for the world.'"

The acidulous pen of Henry L. Mencken also took up the deprecation of democracy. Like Cram, Mencken had no respect for the common man's ability to govern, or even to think. Referring to him invariably as a "boob," a member of the species *"boobus Americanus,"* Mencken challenged the most sacred democratic precepts. Of the yeoman farmer, Jefferson's cornerstone of the republican way, he commented in 1924: "We are asked to venerate this prehensile moron as . . . the citizen *par excellence*, the foundation-stone of the state! . . . To hell with him, and bad luck to him!" Taking up Lippmann's theme Mencken argued that "old fears" and "emotional distractions" prevented the mass of men from reasoning with logic and clarity. Most people, moreover, "are incompetent to take in the bald facts themselves." They suffered from thought-by-stereotype.

In *Notes on Democracy* (1926) Mencken launched his most vigorous attack on popular rule. Democrats, he declared, regarded it as axiomatic that people had the inalienable right to self-government and that they were competent to govern themselves. "The government is called good which responds most quickly and accurately to [the masses'] desires and ideas. That is called bad which conditions their omnipotence and puts a question mark after their omniscience." In Mencken's estimation the only problem with such democratic theory was "that all the known facts lie flatly against it." There was, he continued, no evidence for the wisdom and virtue of the common (Mencken used "inferior") man. Psychology had stripped the old illusions away. "Now we know a great deal more about the content and character of the human mind, . . . and what we have learned has pretty well disposed of the old belief in its congenital intuitions and inherent benevolences." Referring specifically to John B. Watson and behaviorism, Mencken argued that the mere possession of a mind was no guarantee of intelligent political action. Fears and emotions determined behavior from the moment of birth, and most men never escaped their influence far enough to reason clearly. Yet in these minds democrats placed their confidence.

For Mencken the "lower orders of men" had no talent for and no right to self-government. *"Homo vulgaris"* not only lacked intelligence, but a sense of truth, justice, and liberty as well. The average man's laws, customs, and ethics were designed, according to Mencken, to pull down the superior individual to the level of mediocrity.

"I have never encountered any actual evidence," he concluded, "... that *vox populi* is actually *vox Dei*. The proofs, indeed, run the other way."

Still most American intellectuals, Lippmann, Cram, and Mencken included, did not reject democratic ideals in general. It was the particular expression of them in the United States that generated the anger. Democracy, most believed, could be made to work. Even its harshest critics searched for ways of preserving its advantages while avoiding its liabilities. The reason is not hard to find. Democracy had always been more than a political system in American eyes. It was part of the national faith—a way of expressing the individualism that lies at the heart of the national character. As such, democracy embodied basic values which intellectuals of the nervous generation, in particular, were loathe to lose. Far from gleefully burying an old enemy, they lamented the sickness of an old friend and searched for ways to restore his health and usefulness.

Walter Lippmann, for instance, was convinced that the proper medicine for American democracy was the informed, disinterested expert. An intellectual elite composed of specialists in various fields could break the bonds of irrationality and ignorance that frustrated democracy. In *Public Opinion* Lippmann called for the creation of "intelligence bureaus" to be attached to various government departments. The bureaus would also collect and order facts for the public, "interposing some form of expertness between the private citizen and the vast environment in which he is entangled." Experts would make possible mastery rather than drift. A degree of rationality would be injected into political life. The danger of stereotypes would be minimized. Of course the elitism of which Lippmann conceived meant that government would be more *for* the people than *of* and *by* them, but he insisted that his purpose was the improvement of democracy. The experts, in Lippmann's system, would never execute. Their function would be strictly that of advising the people's representatives. In a manner reminiscent of the founding fathers, Lippmann argued that democracy had to be saved from itself by a tempering of the public will.

At the conclusion of *Public Opinion* Lippmann placed a revealing chapter entitled "The Appeal to Reason." Even after accepting so much of Freud's argument for the primacy of the irrational, he returned to reason and intelligence as the best hope of American government. It was not true that reason had failed, but rather that it had not been adequately applied to current political problems. The social sciences were, after all, only in their infancy. With the aid of their objectivity, Lippmann felt that Americans could cultivate a prejudice against prejudice. "There is no ground for ... despair," he concluded. "It is foolish for men to believe, because another great war took place, that intelligence, courage and effort cannot ever contrive a good life for all men." Even "amidst all the evils of this decade [Lippmann was writing in 1922]," some Americans had acted with intelligence and good will. On this fact Lippmann hung his faith in democracy.

In a similar manner, Ralph Adams Cram looked for the revitalization of democracy by an elite leadership. Although this sounded like an argument for oligarchy or even monarchy, Cram explained that elitism held the best hope of "true democracy." Expanding this idea, he distinguished between the "democratic ideal" and the "democratic method." The latter, however, did not necessarily serve the former. "Generally speaking," Cram declared, "the democratic method (unstable, constantly changing its form) is incapable of accomplishing the democratic ideal." If Americans desired the ends of true democracy, "Abolition of Privilege; Equal Opportunity for All; and Utilization of Ability," they would be well advised in Cram's opinion to abandon the deification of the masses and majority rule. Friends of democracy in America since Alexis de Tocqueville had raised the identical warning, and there was no reason to suppose the commentators of the 1920s were less friendly to the cause. War and psychology had rocked the ship of democracy, not sunk it.

As for Henry L. Mencken, he deserves recognition as one of the most misunderstood intellectuals of the 1920s. In almost every account of the period he is represented as an arch-iconoclast, slashing right and left at American values and traditions. Certainly iconoclasm and bitter satire abound in Mencken's writing. But this is not to say he despised everything American. Mencken, in his own way, actually championed the American democratic tradition. His uncompromising opposition to dogma, including that which placed the common man beyond criticism, stemmed from his allegiance to, not his rejection of, the ideal of individual liberty. In this sense Mencken was a democrat. The purpose of much of his writing was to show how far the United States had strayed from the ideals of freedom and democracy. He also suggested a way to recover the trail. The nation needed a "genuine aristocracy," an elite of superior individuals who could govern in such a way as to secure the benefits of democracy without the liabilities. Mencken openly admired the Nietzschean doctrine of supermen. He also praised the way Washington, Hamilton, and Jefferson had created within the republican framework "very ingenious devices for holding the mob in check." These early republicans had shared Mencken's feeling that in regard to liberty too much democracy was worse than too little. He expressed the irony of the situation in the concluding sentence of *Notes on Democracy*: "how can any man be a democrat who is sincerely a democrat?"

It is easy to cull quotations from Mencken that make him appear cynical, even nihilistic, and certainly anti-American. Many commentators, for instance, have seized upon his promise that, if he were elected President, he would dump the Statue of Liberty into the ocean well beyond the three-mile limit. They fail to recognize, however, that in so doing Mencken only intended to keep the real torch of liberty burning vigorously. Statues or their intellectual equivalents —absolutes—only retarded individual freedom and encouraged hypocrisy. Consequently Mencken distrusted anyone who believed in anything too strongly. With himself clearly in mind, he once observed that "the liberation of the human mind has best been furthered by gay fellows who heaved dead cats into sanctuaries and then went roistering down the highways of the world proving to all men that doubt, after all, was safe—that the god in the sanctuary was a fraud. One horselaugh is worth ten thousand syllogisms." Deep down Mencken was a moralist. Yet because he attempted to express his commitment to freedom by using it to the fullest, by attacking every ideal, he has been branded nihilistic. In reality, Mencken was probing and defining the limits of freedom. Positive rather than negative lenses reveal him to be a skillful exponent and staunch defender of the central American traditions of individualism and independent thinking.

On every hand there is evidence that among American intellectuals of the 1920s democratic theory and practice had considerably more vitality than is generally supposed. The American liberal tradition not only survived World War I but in some quarters actually gained strength from the challenge of meeting adversity. Until recently such an assumption verged on the heretical. The custodians of the American past traditionally regarded the 1920s as a reactionary desert between the two shining monuments of twentieth-century American liberalism: Progressivism and the New Deal. Walter Weyl's 1921 characterization of "radicals" like himself as "tired" after "wandering through a wilderness of altruism" before and during the war became a truism. Frederick Hoffman, for instance, contended in 1954 that "American liberalism suffered a serious decline in the years following the war." William E. Leuchtenburg began his 1958 discussion with the question, "What killed progressivism?" But political historians of the 1960s, such as Arthur Link and Otis L. Graham, have led a revision of this estimation. We have been alerted to evidence that the philosophy and politics of liberalism did not wither and die in the twenties.

One group of intellectuals in that decade endeavored to redefine liberty, freedom, and democracy to fit twentieth-century realities. The size and complexity of modern civilization, it was alleged, necessitated the understanding of these concepts in terms of societies rather than individuals. The old individualism had stressed competition and personal freedom; the new emphasized cooperation and social freedom. In describing it intellectuals used the term *social democracy*. The biologist Edwin Grant Conklin explained its meaning in 1921: "the liberty we worship is not, or at least should not be, that of the individual, but rather that of society as a whole—the freedom of nations and races rather than of persons." John Dewey, the preeminent philosopher of social democracy in the 1920s, pointed out that the wilderness conditions of pioneer life had been conducive to personal conquest by creative, rugged individuals. But Dewey, who was in his thirties when Frederick Jackson Turner pronounced the frontier dead in 1892, knew full well that change had made this idea of freedom meaningless, indeed, self-destructive. "It is no longer a physical wilderness that has to be wrestled with," he declared in *Individualism Old and New* (1930). "Our problems grow out of social conditions: they concern human relations rather than man's direct relationship to physical nature."

The new frontier, for Dewey, was a social one. The new democracy, ideally, allowed a man full expression of his individuality within groups, associations, and communities. In *The Public and Its Problems* (1927) he spelled out his hope for the creation of a "Great Community" in the United States. Under this arrangement true democracy would be achieved when the efforts of many individuals, working together, promoted the welfare of everyone in the society. Dewey hedged on the question of what specific political forms the new community would take, but he clearly implied that they would be socialistic. Private property and the free enterprise system, in Dewey's eyes, were institutions befitting circumstances no longer extant in America.

John Dewey's thinking on the subject of democracy in the 1920s represented the attitude of many American intellectuals of his time toward traditional social ideas. While quick to discard what was irrelevant in the pioneer ethos, they retained a firm grasp on the core of American liberalism—a belief in the sanctity of the individual. Their purpose, as Dewey put it, was to prevent "the submergence of the individual" in the bewildering complexities of modern life. In their opinion this demanded radical and ostensibly antidemocratic adjustments. Yet they seemed so only in terms of the old definitions. The changes were really in means rather than ends. In spite of the howls of their critics, the intellectuals in Dewey's camp were interested in preserving, not destroying, democracy. Much of their argument had a familiar ring. Men like T. V. Smith, whose *The Democratic Way of Life* appeared in 1926, and historians Carl Becker, Arthur Schlesinger, Sr., Charles A. Beard, and Vernon Louis Parrington, all of whom published major works in the twenties, walked fully in the paths of eighteenth- and nineteenth-century democrats. It was to be expected that intellectuals and educators like these would not easily surrender confidence in reason, intelligence, and education—the mainstays of the democratic faith.

The idea of social democracy that Dewey articulated bore its most visible fruit during the 1920s in the successful crusade for the public ownership of hydroelectric power and the closely related advent of regional planning. The old and the new liberalism met head on in the controversy over who should control and develop the nation's major rivers. Traditionalists argued on behalf of private enterprise that here was a last frontier to be conquered, as in the past, by rugged individuals. The heirs of progressivism, however, men such as Robert La Follette, Judson King, and especially George W. Norris, challenged this assumption. Rivers, they contended, were communal property which no single person or corporation could legitimately own. Instead water power should be managed by the government in the interest of society as a whole and used to spearhead the renaissance of entire regions. Democracy, it was confidently anticipated, would also be reborn.

The twenties witnessed the climax of the Progressive campaign for multipurpose river development under public auspices. The Water Power Act of 1920 marked a significant forward step, if not a clear victory, for advocates of public ownership. During the subsequent decade movements were begun to commit the federal government to major projects on the St. Lawrence and Columbia rivers. In 1928 the passage of the Swing-Johnson bill authorizing Boulder (later Hoover) Dam made possible the beginning of federally-sponsored environmental engineering on the Colorado. The most dramatic and widely-publicized achievements, however, concerned the Southeast. Beginning in 1921 Senator George W. Norris of Nebraska led a crusade against the attempt of Henry Ford to acquire and develop the Muscle Shoals dam site on the Tennessee River. After blocking Ford's bid, Norris pushed through Congress two bills calling for federal operation of the Muscle Shoals power plant only to see them vetoed by Presidents loyal to private enterprise and suspicious of socialism. Still Norris' efforts kept the option of public development of the Tennessee watershed open. More importantly, they advanced the movement for regional planning that in 1933 resulted in the establishment of the Tennessee Valley Authority.

A product of the 1920s in all but its final enactment, TVA reflected the ideas about democracy prevalent among that decade's intellectuals. It utilized the principle of elitism. Experts and planners would do for the people of the Tennessee valley what they were no longer believed capable of doing for themselves. But at least in the eyes of its proponents TVA was also democratic. Time and again they spoke of grass roots involvement in the project. For David Lilienthal, an early director, TVA was "democracy on the march." Planners and experts, he believed, could in the twentieth century give the people more freedom of choice and more opportunity to control their lives than they could achieve as individuals without TVA. This was precisely the new kind of social democracy of which Dewey spoke. With the aid of science and technology a new era would dawn along the Tennessee. People would progress as societies rather than as individuals.

Expression of the American democratic faith took other forms among intellectuals of the 1920s. A considerable number devoted their efforts to an old-fashioned defense of the individual. Thinking in terms of single persons and personal rights, they championed the little man wherever he seemed in danger of being swamped by bigness or bigotry. The Progressives' method of reforming through politics no longer interested them. Instead they turned to symbolic defenses of basic individual freedoms.

These libertarians had in general opposed American involvement in World War I and particularly the coercion that accompanied the loyalty campaigns. After the war pacifism ceased to be a significant issue, and they turned their attention to other crimes against the individual. The Anti-Defamation League, the National Association for the Advancement of Colored People, and the American Civil Liberties Union were formed to implement their beliefs. Of these groups the ACLU, organized in 1920 from the remnants of the American Union against Militarism, had the most comprehensive program. It proposed to defend through the courts the rights guaranteed by the First Amendment to the Constitution: freedom of speech, press, assembly, and religion. Its motto came from the abolitionist Wendell Phillips: "no matter whose lips speak they must be free and ungagged.... The community which dares not ... is only a gang of slaves." The ACLU's founder and president, Roger Baldwin, believed his organization labored directly in the tradition of Thomas Jefferson. Baldwin and his colleagues continually drew inspiration from the Enlightenment philosophy of natural rights. The ACLU professed confidence in the people's capacity for self-government. It believed in traditional values such as justice, truth, and honor. Jane Addams was typical in her faith in reason, education, and democracy of the town meeting type. She and most other ACLU members supported Robert La Follette's 1924 candidacy for President as a Progressive. What attracted them to the Wisconsin senator was not his specific policies but his moralism and his articulation of old American virtues and ideals. "The political air of Wisconsin," wrote Jane Addams, "filled my lungs like a breath from the mountain tops of the finest American tradition." The "Wisconsin Idea," under which La Follette proposed using experts from the University of Wisconsin to help direct the state's government, also appealed to intellectuals in and out of the ACLU. La Follette appeared to be institutionalizing Lippmann's, Cram's, and Mencken's idea of preserving democracy by tempering it with an injection of expertise.

The total membership of the ACLU during the 1920s was only a thousand, but it included the most prominent liberal and radical intellectuals in the country. Because its purpose—freedom of speech —was so loosely defined, men with widely divergent political, religious, and social ideas could be colleagues within the organization. The gamut ran from the conservative Catholic priest John A. Ryan to liberals like Oswald Garrison Villard, the editor of the *Nation* and grandson of abolitionist William Lloyd Garrison, and on to the leader of the American Communist Party, William Z. Foster. There were lawyers like Clarence Darrow and Felix Frankfurter, muckraking writers such as Upton Sinclair and Ray Stannard Baker, and educators of the stature of Stanford's president David Starr Jordan. Together they participated in a series of defenses of individual rights. The ACLU actually precipitated the Scopes Trial of 1925 by announcing that it would defend any school teacher bold enough to test the Tennessee law prohibiting the teaching of theories contrary to the Biblical account of creation. It also played an important role from 1920 to 1927 in the abortive attempt to extricate foreign-born anarchists Nicola Sacco and Bartolomeo Vanzetti from an allegedly biased judicial system.

The persistence of liberal democratic ideals in the 1920s suggests the need to revise the image of intellectuals in the lost generation as nihilistic, narcissistic, and anti-American. Clearly many did not discard traditional ideals. World War I did not leave the libertarians in the American Civil Liberties Union, for instance, bitter and disillusioned, for the simple reason that they had never expected war to produce peace and brotherhood. Older almost by a generation than the Hemingways and Fitzgeralds, they did not expect miracles overnight. Consequently their vision of the American dream was more durable. Far from being lost after the failures of Progressivism and the strains of wartime, they regrouped in the twenties in defense of libertarian principles. "Radicalism does not die," Roger Baldwin responded in 1926 to an inquiry about the whereabouts of the prewar radicals; "its forms change. The same faith, love of man, that was in the old political reform or social work is now to be found in the labor cause." Recognizing that Progressivism was essentially a moral rather than a political movement, men of this stamp refused to pronounce it dead after 1917. Failure only seems to have inspired greater effort. Democracy also survived the doubts psychology had raised. Sadder but wiser, American liberalism retained sufficient vitality through the 1920s to weather the crises of the subsequent decade.

Nation

A central element in the stereotyped view of the 1920s in America is the idea that intellectuals of the period turned disgustedly against their nation and its past. Puritanism, Victorianism, and babbittry, the standard accounts allege, caused sensitive Americans to seek escape from the cultural wasteland in which they lived. In fact, the opposite was more often the case. Many intellectuals of the twenties displayed a love of nation so strong that it approached bigotry. Too much patriotism, not too little, lay at the root of many of the decade's ugliest aspects. Intellectuals developed the arguments and wrote the books that provided the "scientific" underpinning for racism. In this respect they led rather than fled from popular patriotism and paranoia. A healthier variety of national loyalty produced some of the best poetry and biography of the decade as well as a vigorous interest in historical preservation. Nationalism, in short, flourished in an atmosphere of nervousness. Nicholas Roosevelt expressed a widely held opinion when he wrote in *Current History* in 1929 that "American nationalism has never been so strong."

A systematic philosophy of racism first appeared in American thought during the antebellum justification of slavery. Nourished by European ideas and uneasiness over increasing immigration, racial ideology became widespread in the late nineteenth century. As far as the allegiance of scholars and scientists went, it reached a climax in the 1920s.

The ideology rested on the assumption that a group of people with a common culture and unique history constituted a race. Physical appearance as well as cultural capacity, intelligence, and even morality were thought to be hereditary and congenital. On this basis anthropologists attempted to classify all mankind. Head shape, eye color, and stature were the tools of the trade. As thorough-going evolutionists, the philosophers of race believed that environmental differences produced, over time, physical and cultural variation. Racial distinctiveness, however, was thought to be lost if separate races interbred—the inferior types inevitably adulterating and destroying superior characteristics.

Such ideas appeared repeatedly around the turn of the century in the minds of men like Josiah Strong, Henry Cabot Lodge, and Theodore Roosevelt. World War I served only to heighten the American consciousness of race. The widely publicized intelligence tests administered to army recruits, for example, were taken to prove the existence and relative worth of various racial types. In the post-war decade a group of American intellectuals combined previous evidence with their own growing anxiety into an elaborate theory of race. The importance of their beliefs for the present purpose is that they reflected an intense, if warped, sense of appreciation of and responsibility for the nation.

Madison Grant best represents the racist intellectuals of the twenties. His biographical circumstances are important in understanding his ideas. A member of a wealthy and socially prominent family whose roots extended to the colonial era, Grant stood in the forefront of the eastern establishment. After graduating from Yale in 1887, he trained for the law at Columbia. Grant's legal practice, however, never interfered with his love of hunting, wilderness exploration, and the club life open to a rich, aristocratic bachelor in New York City. He also cultivated an interest in zoology, writing a series of studies about North American animals. In 1895 Grant helped found the New York Zoological Society, one of the purposes of which was to preserve species threatened with extinction. Perhaps this concern led him to think in terms of the decline of human races. At any rate, he soon added ethnology to his interests and began to look with trepidation at immigration.

In 1916 Grant published *The Passing of the Great Race*. The book became the unofficial handbook of racism after the war, and appeared in revised editions in 1918, 1920, and 1921. Its purpose, Grant declared in his 1921 introduction, was "to rouse his fellow Americans to the overwhelming importance of race and to the folly of the 'Melting Pot' theory." America, he explained, had been colonized by people of the Nordic race. Their intellectual and physical superiority over the members of other races largely explained the rapid growth of the United States. Yet the Nordic fathers, according to Grant, made one crucial mistake. They assumed that the New World would produce new men, and consequently welcomed immigrants of all races. Heredity, however, was decisive. Members of inferior races who came to America remained inferior. They threatened, moreover, to dilute and weaken the Nordic strain by interracial breeding. Grant warned that unless the melting pot idea was abandoned and steps taken to preserve racial purity, Nordic supremacy in America and America's supremacy in the world were doomed.

Despite its scholarly trappings, *The Passing of the Great Race* is indisputably wrongheaded both physiologically and historically. It is, nonetheless, a sincerely patriotic work. Grant *loved* his country. He extolled the virtues of the tall, blond, aggressive Nordic pioneers and celebrated the civilization they planted in North America. America and the "native Americans," he insisted, were great. It was only the later, inferior arrivals who had blighted the promise of the young nation. In a typical passage Grant referred to "our Western frontiersmen" as "a far finer type than the settlers who followed them. In fact, it is said that practically every one of the Forty-Niners in California was of Nordic type."

In the preface he wrote for Grant's book, Henry Fairfield Osborn, president of the American Museum of Natural History and a Columbia professor, interpreted the author's frame of mind. "Conservation of that race which has given us the true spirit of Americanism," Osborn writes, "is not a matter either of racial pride or of racial prejudice; it is a matter of love of country." Osborn was overcharitable in exonerating Grant from the charge of racial pride and prejudice, but there is no denying his enthusiasm for the nation and its pioneer past.

Grant did not stop at protest. He was desperately interested in combating the sickness that, in his opinion, endangered his country. Two courses of action seemed available: eugenics and immigration restriction.

Eugenics, or the science of human breeding, had been founded in the 1860s and 1870s by Francis Galton, a cousin of Darwin. Galton argued that exceptional ability was limited to a small number of families and transmitted by heredity to their progeny. This concept led to the idea, which became a near obsession with Madison Grant, of good "stock" or "blood." Eugenicists believed that man could be improved if child bearing were confined to individuals of inherent superiority. Conversely, the breeding of inferior peoples should be restricted. Under no circumstances, it was thought, should superior and inferior races mix because the result would be the perpetuation of the lower type. Thus, Grant pointed out, a white-Negro crossing always produced a Negro and a Nordic-Jewish one a Jew. Brushing aside the objection that environment rather than heredity determined a person's quality, which Franz Boas, a Jewish professor of anthropology, raised, Grant called for the segregation or sterilization of people he regarded as innately inferior. Such measures, as Osborn put it in his preface to *The Passing*, would prevent "the gradual dying out among our people of those hereditary traits through which the principles of our religious, political and social foundations were laid down and their insidious replacement by traits of less noble character." In 1921 the Second International Congress of Eugenics met in New York to publicize this danger and stimulate remedial action. Osborn served the Congress as president; Grant was treasurer. The speakers hammered at the theme of disappearing American traits and ideals, with the more extreme arguing for laws regulating the marriage and procreation of people considered undesirable.

Another way to keep allegedly inferior races from contaminating the original American stock was to confine them to Europe. Madison Grant, for one, was convinced that America's racial malaise had begun with the waves of immigration from southern and eastern Europe after the Civil War. These newcomers, he believed, were racially undesirable relative to the northern and western Europeans who had first settled the New World. Not surprisingly, Grant championed immigration restriction. He applauded the 1910 report of the Immigration (Dillingham) Commission which concluded, in forty-two volumes, that the recent immigrants were inferior to the older types. Even more to Grant's liking were the Literacy Test (1917), the Emergency Quota Act (1921), and the Immigration Act of 1924. The last measure established a quota system, based on national origin, designed to favor Nordics and Anglo-Saxons. Grant himself testified at the congressional hearings which preceded its passage and praised the final law as "our Declaration of Independence" in matters of race. The shutting of the golden door, in his eyes, meant the preservation of American values and the American way of life.

A number of distinguished and influential scholars joined Madison Grant in elaborating the racist formula for "saving" America. From his Harvard chair Professor William McDougall, the most eminent social psychologist of his time, declared in 1921 that indiscriminate racial mixing would initiate the "decline and decay" of American civilization. The Nordic stock (whom McDougall equated with the better classes in American society) should make their own perpetuation their primary concern. Lothrop Stoddard, a geneticist, sociologist, historian, and, like Grant, a lawyer and old-line American feared that the rapid multiplication of inferior races would overwhelm not only the United States but all white civilization. Harvard geneticist Edwin M. East made similar predictions in books published in 1924 and 1927. And throughout the 1920s Frederick A. Woods' *Journal of Heredity* expounded the eugenicists' position.

Of the racist intellectuals who supported Grant the most outspoken on the subject of the American nation was Henry Pratt Fairchild. A professor of sociology at New York University, he published *The Melting-Pot Mistake* in 1926. Its thesis was the familiar one: unrestricted immigration and resulting mongrelization were sapping the vitality of the national character. Fairchild discerned an intellectual as well as a physical dimension to this decline. Foreigners, "imbued with un-American ideas," undermined America's social and political ideology. Almost hysterically, Fairchild called for eugenics and the limitation of immigration.

In his concluding pages Fairchild revealed the source of his concern: intense nationalism. "Among the nations of the world America stands out unique and in many ways preeminent," he declared. "Favored by Nature above all other nations in her physical endowment, favored by history in the character of her people and the type of her institutions, she has a role to play in the development of human affairs which no other nation can play." Explaining this messianic task, Fairchild, like Woodrow Wilson, emphasized the nurture and spread of democracy. Immigrants, however, retarded this process. They could neither comprehend nor participate in the democratic institutions that defined the American mission. As Fairchild put it, "unrestricted immigration . . . was slowly, insidiously, irresistibly eating away the very heart of the United States. What was being melted in the great Melting Pot, losing all form and symmetry, all beauty and character, all nobility and usefulness, was the American nationality itself."

Racist intellectuals like Fairchild and Grant were, in their own way, fervid nationalists. In race mixing they discerned a threat to America's identity and greatness, and they moved to save the nation they loved.

Other varieties of nationalism among intellectuals of the 1920s took less bigoted forms. There were, for one, literary dividends to love of country, and a body of writing emerged in sharp contrast to the deprecations of reputedly alienated intellectuals. A number of writers appreciated what America was and what it was becoming. Rejection of the national tradition, if it occurred at all, was selective. Ralph Waldo Emerson might be out of favor, but not Walt Whitman. Certain aspects of contemporary civilization might displease, but a faith in the nation's central core persisted.

Carl Sandburg illustrates the point. Born on the western Illinois prairie, Sandburg fell in love with America before the 1920s and maintained his affection right through the decade. In a vigorous free verse style, Sandburg celebrated the vitality and power he sensed in both the pioneer past and urban present of his country. The prairie, he wrote in 1918, "gave me a song and a slogan" while Chicago was a "City of the Big Shoulders," the heir of the frontier's strength. This sense of transference freed Sandburg from the misgivings with which other Americans of his time viewed the ending of the pioneer era. He looked to the nation's future with a confidence surprising to those who have taken T. S. Eliot's prediction of the way the world would end ("not with a bang but a whimper") as typical of the twenties. In 1928 Sandburg wrote: "you have kissed good-by to one century, one little priceless album. [You will yet kiss good-by to ten, twenty centuries. Ah! you shall have such albums!] ... Good morning, America!" That this future would be one of *Smoke and Steel,* the title of a 1920 collection, rather than *Cornhuskers* (1918) bothered Sandburg not at all. America's wilderness heritage would nourish the nation as it grew and changed. In a manner reminiscent of Whitman, Sandburg used the geographic magic of the United States to create metaphors for this idea: "There is an eagle in me and a mockingbird ... and the eagle flies along the Rocky Mountains of my dreams and fights among the Sierra crags of what I want ... and the mockingbird warbles in the early forenoon before the dew is gone, warbles in the underbrush of my Chattanoogas of hope, gushes over the blue Ozark foothills of my wishes – And I got the eagle and the mockingbird from the wilderness."

Sandburg's affirmation of America and its people carried over from his verse to his other literary endeavors. In 1927 he published *The American Songbag,* a collection of native ballads and folk songs. Unlike the racists, he accepted the heterogeneity of America's folk tradition as an asset. Most of Sandburg's creative talents in the 1920s were devoted to a monumental biography of Abraham Lincoln. *Abraham Lincoln: The Prairie Years* appeared in 1926 in two heavy volumes; the last four, *The War Years,* thirteen years later. From the standpoint of scholarship Sandburg's books had many defects. Yet his purpose was less historical documentation than imaginative embodiment of a cherished American myth. Like the bards of old, Sandburg used his protagonist to fashion a national epic. If the result was a larger-than-life Lincoln, it was also a sincere expression of faith and love.

The preeminent American epic of the 1920s, Stephen Vincent Benét's *John Brown's Body* (1928), also has a Civil War setting. The circumstances of Benét's life seemed to earmark him for a lost generation. He was indisputably a young intellectual, only twenty-two in 1920, and a product of private preparatory schools and Yale University. He even went to Paris in 1920 and wrote a novel. But Benét resisted alienation; more exactly, he never considered it. He married happily and permanently, had two children, wrote lyrical tributes to his native land, and became highly popular before the close of the twenties as an articulator of pride and patriotism.

The first published indication of Benét's feeling for America was his 1922 *Ballad of William Sycamore.* He used the poem to paint an idealized picture of a frontiersman. Sycamore has a clean, free grace and a rapport with nature—both products of his wilderness environment. In Sandburg's manner Benét drew deeply on American history and legend to write the ballad, and his affection for them is apparent on every page.

Benét returned to Paris in 1926 to write *John Brown's Body*, but only because he believed he could make his Guggenheim Fellowship go further there than in the more expensive United States. His loyalties never wavered. "Living abroad," he wrote in 1928, "has intensified my Americanism." *John Brown's Body* attempted to express this feeling. While the book-length poem was in progress he stated his expectations for it in a letter to his publisher: "I hope it has in it some of the landscapes, sights, the sounds of the people which are American. I am tired, not of criticism of America, for no country can be healthy without self-criticism, but of the small railers, conventional rebels. We also have a heritage—and not all of it wooden money." Benét personally likened his efforts to those of Joel Barlow, an untalented if prolific epic poet of the early national period, but his admirers less modestly compared his achievement to that of Homer and Virgil and helped him win a Pulitzer Prize in 1928.

John Brown's Body treats the lives of dozens of characters, common people as well as national leaders, against the background of the Civil War. It is full of the magic Benét sensed in America's environment and civilization. Its symbolism and language are distinctively native. Its philosophy rests on traditional American values like freedom and individualism. Indeed in his "Invocation" to the poem Benét sets forth his intent to court the "American muse" and capture "the pure elixer, the American thing." The end result approaches this ideal as closely as any literature of the present century. An intellectual of the supposedly alienated twenties, Benét created a paean to his country and a milestone in the emergence of a national style.

The life and thought of Hart Crane present a variation in the theme of nationalism. Unlike Sandburg and Benét, Crane definitely experienced doubt and uncertainty during the 1920s. In April 1928 he observed that "the spiritual disintegration of our period becomes more painful to me every day, so much so that I now find myself baulked by doubt at the validity of practically every metaphor that I coin." But Crane still endeavored to fashion metaphors suggesting America's underlying spiritual vitality. His nervous uncertainty seemed to goad him to greater efforts at affirmation. From 1923 to 1929 he wrote *The Bridge.* A long, intricate poem, it was the vehicle for Crane's search for what he termed "the Myth of America." He sought to affirm his country—not only its pioneer past but its urban, industrial present. According to Crane there was spiritual nourishment in technological productions such as the Brooklyn Bridge. He celebrated the courage, faith, and skill that had spanned New York's East River and built modern American civilization. The pessimism of Eliot and Spengler was not for Hart Crane. More exactly, he felt the force of pessimism but tried to resist it. The fact that he failed (he died a suicide in 1932) does not detract from the sincerity of his effort. In many ways Crane typified intellectuals of the nervous generation in his hunger for solid values. He also represented the many who looked for such values in the American nation.

Another manifestation of nationalism in the twenties was a concern on the part of many intellectuals for the preservation of the past. Perhaps because of their relatively short history, Americans have coveted tangible evidence of national tradition. The historic preservation movement began on a major scale in the 1850s with the acquisition of George Washington's home at Mount Vernon as a national shrine. It gathered momentum in the 1890s when both the American Scenic and Historic Preservation Society and the Society for the Preservation of New England Antiquities were founded. But the greatest acceleration of the movement took place in the 1920s. Fear that evidence and memory of the past might be obliterated by modern civilization compelled the crusade. So did a desire to stimulate patriotism. And many believed that historic preservation would fortify the Puritan ethic of work, denial, faith, and fortitude— the very puritanism that has been regarded as anathema to the twenties. In other words, for every American who deprecated the influence of Puritans and pioneers on the national character, there was at least one other concerned about saving an old New England home or a frontier village.

Historic preservation had widespread appeal among thoughtful Americans of the twenties. In Philadelphia the Colonial Chain, five homes restored between 1925 and 1927, became the subject of considerable community pride. As the president of the Philadelphia Historical Society declared in 1924, such preservation mattered because "the acts of an honest, virtuous, and pious people ... were worthy of commemoration." Those who lacked "burning patriotism," he continued, should be exposed to historic sites where "their hearts will throb and their eyes grow dim." Old Deerfield Village in Massachusetts was such a place, as was Monticello in Virginia which the Thomas Jefferson Memorial Society bought in 1925.

The most prominent preservation projects undertaken in the twenties were made possible by large-scale philanthropy. In 1927 Henry Francis du Pont began to collect the antique furnishings that eventually adorned the Winterthur Museum. "I am ... glad that I have been able to preserve in some degree the evidences of early life in America," du Pont remarked, "and I am gratified to feel that others may find in my collection a source of knowledge and inspiration." The Rockefeller restoration of Williamsburg, Virginia, also began in the middle of the decade. The motto of Colonial Williamsburg, Inc., "That the Future May Learn From the Past," expressed the motivation of John D. Rockefeller, Jr., and his associates. In New England the major force for preservation was William Sumner Appleton and his Society for the Preservation of New England Antiquities. A proper Bostonian in every sense and an intellectual by any definition, Appleton would have none of alienation from country. Instead he devoted his considerable wealth, influence, and energy to protecting colonial homes in the Boston area. Appleton also became a kind of clearing-house for preservation activities throughout the East, and had the satisfaction of seeing the S.P.N.E.A. grow by 1923 to almost three thousand members.

Like Rockefeller, Henry Ford also undertook the preservation of an entire community, Greenfield Village, Michigan, for revealing reasons (see Chapter V), but concern for the past extended beyond millionaires. Americans of taste and culture but of average means could collect antiques. Their purpose was not simply esthetic. As the magazine of the Daughters of the American Revolution observed in 1927, "the patriotic Americans who treasure the memory of our forefathers can do no better today than to reproduce in their homes the furniture and decorations [of historic times]."

Nationalism had a variety of outlets during the 1920s. Underlying them all, however, was a sense of pride in being American. This essential unity is illustrated in the career of Kenneth Roberts during the postwar decade. In 1920 Roberts received an assignment from the *Saturday Evening Post* to go to Europe and study emigration. The resulting articles, published in the magazine and separately as *Why Europe Leaves Home* (1922), followed Madison Grant's Nordic supremacy argument. Roberts assumed that the original American stock was good. But the flood of immigrants from southern and eastern Europe was producing in the United States "a hybrid race of people as worthless and futile as the good-for-nothing mongrels of Central America and Southeastern Europe." By the late twenties, however, Roberts' nationalism had taken a different form. In 1930 he published the first of his many historical novels—*Arundel*, a story of the American Revolution. The book mythologized the American past; great men and glorious deeds filled its pages. In his role as racist as well as novelist Kenneth Roberts revealed an enthusiasm for the nation quite contrary to the standard assessment of the twenties.

Nature

"Was there ever a time in human history," John C. Van Dyke asked in 1920, "when a return to Nature was so much needed as just now? How shall the nations be rebuilded, the lost faith and hope renewed, the race live again save through the Great Mother whom we have forsaken?" While exceptionally lavish in his praise, Van Dyke was not alone in his opinion of nature. In various ways many intellectuals of the postwar decade evinced a deep commitment to natural values and a determination to do something about asserting their influence in American life. This appreciation of nature was closely related to the appreciation of nation. Indeed many of the most ardent racists and immigration restrictionists were active in crusades to protect nature. The desire to save the distinctively American environment (the frontier) blended easily with a concern about maintaining the purity of the original racial stock and the integrity of American traditions. Madison Grant, for instance, was president of the Boone and Crocket Club, an organization devoted to the protection and appreciation of big game, its wilderness habitat, and the virile skills required for its pursuit. Grant also participated in the founding of the Save-the-Redwoods League in 1918 and served on the boards of the National Parks Association and the American Bison Society. Likewise Henry Fairfield Osborn, president of the American Museum of Natural History and a prominent eugenicist, was involved in saving both nation and nature.

Americans between twenty and forty years of age in the 1920s were the first generation to have grown to maturity without the presence of a frontier on the edges of their civilization. After three centuries of expansion there was no longer sufficient wilderness to create a frontier situation. Indeed nature seemed in danger of being overwhelmed. Urbanization and industrialization were transforming the American environment. In 1920 the census revealed that for the first time a majority (51.2 per cent) of Americans lived in cities of 2,500 or more. In the twenties alone New York City grew 23 per cent, Detroit 57 per cent, and Los Angeles 115 per cent. Automobiles had been curiosities when the twentieth century began, but by 1920 over nine million were registered. At the end of the decade the figure was twenty-seven million. For many these were discomforting phenomena. Especially among intellectuals, nature had long been held in high esteem. It had seemed to many that the possession of large quantities of wild nature was America's badge of distinctiveness and assurance of vitality. Nature also served as an inspiration to art and morality. And wilderness conditions were thought to underlie and sustain cherished American values. Accepting the thesis of Frederick Jackson Turner, many agreed with Carl Becker's reasoning: "if American institutions and ideals... have been the result of primitive frontier conditions, it would seem that they must, with the passing of those conditions, be transformed into something different—perhaps altogether different."

Anxiety over urbanization prompted a surge of concern for extending the influence of nature in American life. One of the most creative and prophetic thinkers on this subject in the 1920s was Benton MacKaye, the father of environmental planning. As early as 1921 MacKaye expressed alarm over the disappearance of the natural environment in the United States. His home near Boston provided an excellent vantage point from which to observe the spread of urban conditions. It seemed to him that the nation was threatened with the prospect of becoming one huge city. The metropolis was like a flood, flowing across the passes and through the valleys, consuming what MacKaye called the "indigenous world." He foresaw the time when Americans would be unable to find substantial areas of undeveloped nature in which to escape the pressures of civilization.

In 1928 Benton MacKaye offered his solution for resisting the urbanizing force in a book entitled *The New Exploration: A Philosophy of Regional Planning*. Explaining his title, MacKaye declared that the "old exploration" concerned the extraction of raw material from the environment, the conquest of the wilderness. The American pioneer had carried the brunt of this exploitative task, and it had served his needs. But the cultured man of the post-pioneering era could not exist on bread alone. He demanded, according to MacKaye, that the environment do more than just keep him alive; it had to bring him joy. True living, as opposed to mere existing, depended on the presence of an environment capable of satisfying man's spiritual needs. For too long, MacKaye contended, Americans had construed natural resources to mean only economic goods like lumber and coal. The natural world, however, was replete with esthetic, inspirational, and educational values. These, too, were resources and ones of vital importance to the welfare of a civilization. MacKaye's new exploration aimed at defining these values and making them available to twentieth-century Americans through regional planning.

The idea that America could become overcivilized was not new with Benton MacKaye. Henry David Thoreau, John Muir, and Theodore Roosevelt, among others, had pointed to this possibility before 1920. But the spurt in technology and urbanization that accompanied and followed World War I made it increasingly real. Intellectuals, in particular, were concerned because they sensed that the preservation of natural values was a way of tempering the American obsession with utility and commerce. Consequently MacKaye attracted attention with his idea that the flood of civilization emanating from the cities could be "dammed" or "dyked" by strips of open, undeveloped land. These wilderness or natural areas around and between the nation's major urban centers "would divide . . . the flood waters of metropolitanism into separate 'basins' and thereby tend to avert their complete and total confluence." MacKaye argued that city people needed this "system of open ways" as a sanctuary from the strains of "an overmechanical civilization." Ranges of hills and mountains were the logical places to begin holding the line against development. In 1921, seven years before publishing *The New Exploration*, MacKaye had called for the establishment and protection of a belt of wild land running along the crest of the Appalachian Mountains from Maine to Georgia. His idea bore fruit in the successful movement for the Appalachian Trail.

MacKaye concluded his 1928 discussion with a warning: America was "the most 'volcanic' of any area on earth." The nation, in his opinion, had a high potential for bitterness, for violence, and for "deep domestic strife." Dissatisfied citizens could tear the country apart. Nature was needed as a pacifying influence, a source of recreation and recuperation. Environmental planning was needed to provide nature in sufficient quantity to satisfy an increasingly civilized people.

Appreciation of nature enjoyed unprecedented support in the 1920s. A number of voices singled out wilderness as the original American environment. Emerson Hough, the novelist whose historical romance *The Covered Wagon* (1922) became a motion picture, expressed his ideas in the *Saturday Evening Post*. Over two million Americans read his impassioned plea in January 1922 for the preservation of Arizona's forested Kaibab Plateau immediately north of the Grand Canyon. Hough began his article with a paean to the beauty of the virgin continent. A diatribe against careless exploitation of the nation's natural assets followed: "we have sold our fresh beauty of youth on the open streets—and cheap, so ghastly cheap."

Most commentators on the 1920s contend that the intellectuals of that time abandoned hope in the face of philistinism and retreated to private cursing of the ascendancy of babbitry. Hough, however, does not support this generalization. He was prepared to fight for nature and for beauty against commercialism, and he believed he could win. In his arsenal were ideas long a part of the American discussion of nature but given new urgency by the rapid disappearance of wilderness. The Kaibab forest, he argued, was "the grandest natural work of Almighty God now left in all the world!"

Its preservation for future generations would create "the most magnificent heirloom any nation ever gave her children." Connecting nation and nature, Hough called for the protection of a "typical portion of the American wilderness" that could show citizens "what the old America once was, how beautiful, how splendid."

By the 1920s thoughtful Americans were widely bemoaning the disappearance of the frontier and of pioneering. Most took for granted the logic of Frederick Jackson Turner, who, in a book published in 1920 (but written at various times in the preceding three decades) observed that "the ... rough conquest of the wilderness is accomplished, and that great supply of free lands which year after year has served to reinforce the democratic influences in the United States is exhausted." Inevitably, Turner wondered if American ideals and institutions "have acquired sufficient momentum to sustain themselves under conditions so radically unlike those in the days of their origin?" Others, with similar doubts, searched for solutions. Theodore Roosevelt, the son of the President, agreed that pioneering shaped the American character. But, he wrote in 1924, "now our frontier is gone" and an unaccustomed softness is apparent in American life. "Sturdy self-reliance, simplicity, and courage," warned Roosevelt, must be protected or they too would vanish. One way was to encourage manly outdoor activities that would bring Americans into close contact with nature. With this in mind Roosevelt personally inspired a National Conference on Outdoor Recreation in 1924. The 309 delegates who gathered in Washington, D.C., heard President Calvin Coolidge say "the physical vigor, moral strength, and clean simplicity of mind of the American people can be immeasurably furthered by the properly developed opportunities for the life in the open afforded by our forests, mountains, and waterways. Life in the open," Coolidge went on, "is a great character builder. From such life much of the American spirit of freedom springs."

Other speakers at the 1924 conference detailed the advantages of contact with wilderness. Camping, hunting, and fishing, it was pointed out, were "the American heritage" and sorely in need of encouragement in an urbanizing age. In 1926 the nation's foremost thinkers on the subject of nature and recreation assembled for a second national conference. Speech after speech in praise of nature ensued. Herbert Hoover, for one, spoke of the growing need "to return to the primitive life in the mountains, woods, and streams. In our outdoor life," he added, "we do get repose from the troubles of soul that this vast complex of civilization imposes upon us." Hoover, an ardent fisherman, concluded by recommending angling as an antidote to urbanism.

At first glance it seems surprising that in the 1920s so many city-oriented intellectuals appreciated the natural world. Actually the urban situation of increasing numbers of Americans contributed to the growing vogue of the nature movement. Cut off from contact with the land, people longed for it. The pioneer, in a sense, had too much nature to covet it, but the city-dweller reached out for what was rare and, consequently, precious. "I propose," wrote the Cornell botanist and sociologist Liberty Hyde Bailey in 1918, "a Society of the Holy Earth. . . . Its principle of union will be the love of the Earth, treasured in the hearts of men and women. To every person who longs to walk on bare ground, who stops in a busy day for the song of a bird, . . . and who would escape self-centered, commercial and physical valuations of life . . . to all these souls everywhere the call will come." Bailey and those whose ideas he represented did not want to revert permanently to caves and skins. Rather they sought a middle way between nature and civilization. They hoped to avoid the liabilities of an urban age while securing its advantages. This desire gave rise to an admiration of arcadia—the pastoral midpoint between the wild and the civilized. Popularity of the suburban way of life followed. New York City had no less than 129 incorporated suburbs by 1925, most of which had appeared since World War I. One of the most famous, Radburn, New Jersey, featured ample park and grassland according to the garden city model. The ideal, as articulated by Lewis Mumford and other antiurbanists, was a happy marriage of town and country, civilization and wilderness. The nation could progress without losing hold of sacred natural values. Old farms, in New England especially, or summer cottages also attracted intellectuals as retreats. But some turned to them, in Mumford's 1925 words, "not as a temporary refuge but as a permanent seat of life and culture, urban in its advantages, permanently rural in its situation." One such neopioneer was Ralph Borsodi who in 1920 moved his family from New York City to a subsistence farm and later chronicled the economic and emotional benefits in *Flight from the City.*

At Vanderbilt University in Nashville, Tennessee, in the early 1920s a group of young southern writers developed a full-bodied philosophy of agrarianism. Turning their backs on the New South of mills, railroads, and cities, they deified the old rural environment.

Nature, in their opinion, was in league with innocence, simplicity, tradition, completeness, and, consequently, with religion, art, letters, and the good life. The old, antebellum South knew this well, but the nation had opted for, and with the Civil War enforced, the northern Yankee way. Now Americans, South as well as North, were in danger of losing the essential contact with the natural world. Urbanization, according to Donald Davison, had removed modern man so far from the land as to make him forget that "the chief subject of art, in the final sense, is nature."

In 1930 twelve of the Nashville agrarians collaborated on a book: *I'll Take My Stand.* As their opening manifesto made clear, they stood for the idea that the past, closer to nature, had been better than the urban-industrial present. John Crowe Ransome explained how the doctrine of progress had caused Americans to "wage an unrelenting war on nature." It was preferable, he argued, to conclude a truce and "live on terms of mutual respect and amity" as earlier agrarian societies had done. But the United States had taken the other route and attempted to dominate nature. The unfortunate results were visible on every hand. Perhaps Andrew Nelson Lytle's best summarized the agrarian intellectuals' message. "A farm is not a place to grow wealthy," he protested; "it is a place to grow corn."

Nostalgic yearning for simpler ways appeared in surprising places. Many New York City intellectuals lived in an informal district within the metropolis called, significantly, Greenwich Village. They coveted its informality and the way it humanized the big city. The scale of the Village in the twenties did not dwarf man in either a literal or figurative sense. Floyd Dell caught its magic in verse:

> Where now the tide of traffic beats,
> There was a maze of crooked streets;
> The noisy ways of enterprise,
> Swift-hurrying to their destinies,
> Swept past this island paradise:
> Here life went to a gentler pace,
> And dreams and dreamers found a place.

It was even possible to tend small gardens in the backyards of the Village brownstone apartments, and for those anxious to find respite from the problems of modern urban America, this was a precious opportunity.

Yet for some the pastoral or village environment was insufficient.

Pushed by their discontent with modern society and pulled by the call of the wild, they sought the primitive—in idea if not always in fact. In the wilderness was total escape from civilization, a way of keeping alive the old pioneer skills and values, and a means of finding esthetic and spiritual satisfaction. The wilderness preservation movement rode the wave these ideas generated. Intellectuals in the twenties took considerable interest in resisting the assault of an expanding civilization on the remaining American wilderness.

The foremost champion of wild country in the 1920s was Aldo Leopold, a profound philosopher of man's relationship to nature, who cut the channels in which a large portion of American thought on this subject subsequently flowed. In 1909, with degrees from Yale and the Yale Forest School in his pocket, Leopold joined the United States Forest Service. A decade of work on the National Forests of Arizona and New Mexico convinced him, first, of the importance of preserving wilderness and, second, of the need to do it quickly before the nation's remaining wild country vanished under the growing demand for raw materials. In 1921 Leopold published an article in the *Journal of Forestry* with the object of giving "definite form to the issue of wilderness conservation." He proposed that a large tract of Forest Service land at the headwaters of New Mexico's Gila River be reserved exclusively for wilderness recreation. Many shook their heads at Leopold's defiance of professional forestry's traditional utilitarianism, but in 1924 he succeeded in persuading his superior to designate over a half-million acres as the Gila Primitive Area. Leopold realized, however, that the fight to preserve wilderness was in its infancy. A convincing rationale was needed, and in 1925 he published three articles setting forth the case for wilderness.

"Conserving the Covered Wagon," which appeared in *Sunset* in March, pointed out that for most young Americans the frontier was already unreal. Future generations would know even less about pioneer conditions. "If we think we are going to learn by cruising around the mountains in a Ford," Leopold made clear, "we are largely deceiving ourselves." In *American Forests and Forest Life* for October 1925, Leopold continued with this theme: "we have come to the end of our pioneer environment and are about to push its remnants into the Pacific. For three centuries that environment has determined the character of our development; it may, in fact, be said that, coupled with the character of our racial stocks, it is the very stuff America is made of. Shall we now exterminate this thing that made us American?"

In his third 1925 article Leopold answered this question himself. He began his argument with the contention that "many of the attributes most distinctive of America and Americans are [due to] the impress of the wilderness and the life that accompanied it." Explaining, he continued: "if we have such a thing as an American culture (and I think we have), its distinguishing marks are a certain vigorous individualism, combined with ability to organize, a certain intellectual curiosity bent to practical ends, a lack of subservience to stiff social forms, and an intolerance of drones, all of which are distinctive characteristics of successful pioneers. These, if anything, are the indigenous part of our Americanism, the qualities that set it apart as a new rather than an imitative contribution to civilization." Finally, Leopold drew the conclusion that Frederick Jackson Turner only implied: "is it not a bit beside the point for us to be so solicitous about preserving [American] institutions without giving so much as a thought to preserving the environment which produced them and which may now be one of our effective means of keeping them alive?" Wilderness preserves, then, were not just for fun. They maintained the opportunity for successive generations of Americans to acquaint themselves firsthand with the conditions that shaped their character and culture.

In 1928 Leopold left the Forest Service to pursue a brilliant career as an ecologist and wildlife manager. His conceptions of a "land ethic" and an "ecological conscience" marked a broadening of concern from wilderness to the natural world in general. Although articulated in publications of the 1930s and 1940s, the roots of Leopold's attitude go back to the previous decades. From Liberty Hyde Bailey's *The Holy Earth* (1915) he learned that, because God created it, the natural world was divine. It followed that man's abuse of the earth was not only economically unsound but morally wrong. It was necessary, Bailey wrote, to overcome "cosmic selfishness" and develop a sense of "earth righteousness." This would transfer man's relationship to nature from the realm of commerce to that of morals. Albert Schweitzer's "reverence for life" philosophy, with which Leopold was familiar, had a similar import. Leopold's "land ethic" carried such ideas into the twenties and beyond. Conservation, according to Leopold, was not efficient exploitation or wise use but rather a policy which preserved the "integrity, stability, and beauty" of the natural world. An "ecological conscience," in his view, "changes the role of *Homo sapiens* from conquerer of the land-community to plain member and citizen of it." Far from rejecting nature as a national value, the work of Leopold and his fellow ecologists provided new reasons for respecting it.

Aldo Leopold's crusade for wilderness received increasing support through the 1920s from far-sighted scientists, planners, and administrators. Arthur H. Carhart, a recreation officer with the Forest Service, insisted that contact with wild country made the average American "a better citizen, mentally, physically and spiritually." Wilderness, after all, was "God's world"; civilization merely man's. For Frank A. Waugh, a professor of landscape architecture and Forest Service adviser, "outdoor recreation is a necessity of civilized life, and as civilization becomes more intensive the demand grows keener." Providing nature, Waugh declared as early as 1918, was just as legitimate a use of the National Forests as providing lumber.

Chief Forester William B. Greeley initially had some doubts on this point, but by 1927 he too accepted the preservation of wilderness as desirable. In an article entitled "What Shall We Do with Our Mountains?" he questioned the wisdom of conquering the wilderness completely. Like Leopold, Greeley combined love of nature with love of nation: "our national development has always had a background, or setting, of forest and frontier. . . . It has created many cherished traditions and national heroes . . . [and has] probably been the greatest single factor in molding our sturdier national qualities since the colonists landed on the Atlantic Coast." Greeley was in a position to do more than write. In 1929 the Forest Service established an administrative policy of preserving wilderness on selected parts of the National Forests.

It remained for Robert Marshall to cap the 1920s with a ringing defense of the place of wilderness in American civilization. His statement appeared in *Scientific Monthly* for February 1930. Marshall completely contradicts the lost generation stereotype. He was a young intellectual (nineteen in 1920, the product of private eastern universities, author, and Ph.D.), and he was extremely wealthy thanks to the efforts of his famous lawyer-father. He could easily have chosen the life of dissipation and debunking widely attributed to the rich and smart of the twenties. But instead Marshall elected to define and defend traditional values and to live the life of outdoorsman with a zest one would suppose was reserved for partakers of bathtub gin. For Marshall the basic importance of wild nature was its capacity for meeting human needs that civilization left unsatisfied. Health—"soundness, stamina, and élan"—was one; beauty, another. But the greatest values of wilderness were mental. Marshall drew directly on Sigmund Freud in arguing that many persons needed occasional release from the repressive effects of civilization if they were to avoid neuroses and insanity. Wilderness offered them wholesome excitement, peace, and, above all, freedom. Following the insights into sublimation suggested by William James, Marshall contended that people denied the thrill and challenge of wilderness would turn to "equivalents" such as crime and war.

Robert Marshall concluded his 1930 manifesto with a ringing appeal to Americans to join him in a "fight for the freedom of the wilderness." The Wilderness Society, a citizen action and pressure group, resulted. Thanks to Marshall's generous financial support and indefatigable zeal, the Wilderness Society and wilderness preservation generally made substantial gains in the 1930s.

The American discussion of national parks in the 1920s was widespread, penetrating, and enthusiastic. The twenties, in fact, saw the rise of esthetic conservation or preservation become a major challenge to utilitarian conservation. The nerve center for the nature lovers was the National Park Service and its driving force, Stephen T. Mather. A millionaire manufacturer and Sierra Club mountaineer, Mather became the first director of the Service in 1916 and remained in that capacity until 1929. A master of public relations, he succeeded spectacularly in selling the parks to the American people. Attendance figures at all the parks rose from 250,000 in 1914 to 1,000,000 in 1920 and 2,500,000 in 1928. This increase, to be sure, reflected the advent of the automobile age, but it also testified to the effectiveness of Mather and his colleagues in convincing Americans of the value of national parks.

Men with ideas and the ability to express them contributed significantly to this campaign for public sympathy and government support. One of Mather's first acts as director of the National Park Service was to recruit Robert Sterling Yard, a veteran newspaperman, to take charge of publicizing the parks. Yard believed that "anything that makes strongly for the physical and mental health of the people, for pride of country, ... for travel, recreation, and recuperation, makes powerfully for individual and national fitness to carry on and up the nation's material progress." Nature, then, had utilitarian as well as esthetic advantages. To get this message across, Yard wrote and circulated thousands of lavishly illustrated brochures, books, pamphlets, and maps. He encouraged national magazines to stress the park theme with spectacular results. The *Annual Report* of the National Park Service recorded that between September 1916 and October 1917 over three hundred articles appeared in ninety-five journals. The figures for the next several years were equally impressive. While neither original nor profound, these publications revealed a continuing, indeed accelerating, recognition of the value of nature.

For Enos Mills, a guide in the Colorado Rockies and author of *Your National Parks* (1917), the parks preserved "a bit of the primeval world and the spirit of the vigorous frontier." They would help "keep the nation young"—a relevant task in a society conscious of becoming middle aged. According to Mills, national parks were not concerned with saving nature so much as saving people. They provided "glorious room . . . in which to find ourselves, in which to think and hope, to dream and plan, to rest and resolve." Generalizing beyond the American situation, Mills concluded: "without parks and outdoor life all that is best in civilization will be smothered."

Probably the most important intellectual to support the national park movement in the twenties was John C. Merriam, distinguished paleontologist, president of the Carnegie Institution, prolific author and lecturer, and unofficial dean of American nature lovers. From its founding in 1918 Merriam was one of the mainstays of the National Parks Association, a citizen group Robert Sterling Yard had organized to promote and defend the parks. He also advised the Secretary of the Interior on park problems and, during the twenties, was the driving force in initiating interpretive programs, lectures, and museums in the national parks. In addition Merriam served as president of the Save-the-Redwoods League, justified wildlife conservation, and championed outdoor recreation at the national conferences of 1924 and 1926. Like many intellectuals of the time, Merriam conceived of the parks as educational resources—"super universities" for the study of natural phenomena and the wonder of life. "The work of the Creator's hand," he declared in 1927, "presents itself here in such a way that all may comprehend." The national parks were "regions where one looks through the veil to meet the realities of nature and of the unfathomable power behind it." If this sounds like Ralph Waldo Emerson, it is only another piece of evidence that many American intellectuals of the 1920s professed quite traditional values.

Serious fiction in the twenties also reflected enthusiasm for nature. Many writers apparently turned to it as a spiritual gyroscope from which to derive stability and strength. Frequently preoccupation with nature stemmed from disenchantment with modern civilization. Thus in the famous conclusion of *The Great Gatsby* (1925), F. Scott Fitzgerald's protagonist muses with rhapsodic wonder on the "fresh, green breast of the new world" that contrasts so sharply with West Egg decadence. Ernest Hemingway's 1924 short story "Big Two-Hearted River" similarly juxtaposes the tranquility of a trout stream with the nerve-cracking strain of a war-torn world. The implication is that man desperately needs contact with nature to restore his perspective and his faith. In *The Sun Also Rises* (1926) Hemingway has Jake Barnes find a momentary oasis of beauty and value fishing in the Spanish Pyrenees. As Hemingway put it in his famous sparse style, "it felt good lying on the ground." People close to the ground were also good. Hemingway made much of the simple strength and dignity of the Spanish peasants. Contact with nature seemed to invest their lives with a coveted naturalness.

The most persistent exponent of nature in American letters during the twenties was Willa Cather of Greenwich Village. Beginning in 1913 with *O Pioneers!* and continuing through *My Antonia* (1918) and *Death Comes for the Archbishop* of 1927, she extolled the virtue of closeness to the land. The earlier novels concerned frontier Nebraska of the 1880s and earth goddesses like Antonia Shimerda. In the mid-1920s Cather turned to the Southwest. She loved this vast country and seemed, as one critic put it, "to hang over the landscape with something of the tenderness of its own early summer sky." But Cather eschewed romanticism and sentimentality in her attitude toward nature. The desert wilderness was often harsh, inhospitable, overpowering. Still it possessed a durability, a vitality, and a tranquility that those who knew it could absorb. Modern civilization disgusted Willa Cather for its lack of these qualities. Yet she refused to be lost. Her mind was anchored by the genteel tradition, the past, the church (she became an Episcopalian in 1922 and wrote with respect of Roman Catholicism), and, especially, nature. With these guidelines she moved confidently if sadly through the twenties.

The poet Robinson Jeffers offers an extreme example of how the rejection of civilization could lead to love of nature. His disgust with man was profound. The only solace was the natural scene— particularly the golden hills and rugged surf-pounded rocks of California's Big Sur coast. There Jeffers found escape in the permanence and grandeur so singularly lacking in man's world. Much of Jeffers' poetry in the twenties is a savage catalog of human depravity. "But look," he wrote in a 1927 collection, "how noble the world is, / The lonely flowing water, / the secret- / Keeping stones, the flowing sky." Civilized society might by disintegrating, man might be hopelessly imperfect, but nature was eternal. For Jeffers and many of his fellow intellectuals of the 1920s the natural world was insurance against becoming lost.

Esthetics

American criteria of the beautiful underwent such sharp changes in the second and third decades of the twentieth century that it could be said a cultural revolution occurred. Old canons of taste, style, and form were thrust aside as creative impulses sought freedom of expression. Few of the arts escaped untouched from the esthetic ferment. The upshot was a cultural explosion in the American 1920s. In literature, for example, few ten-year periods have ever produced so much significant work. The first American to receive a Nobel Prize for literature, Sinclair Lewis, won the award at the end of the decade. The rebellious spirit of the twenties led intellectuals toward innovation and artistic achievement rather than despair and dissipation. Artists of the time showed a willingness to throw off provincial attitudes, depart from European standards, and push forward the quest for cultural nationalism. Indeed R. L. Duffus' *The American Renaissance,* a 1928 survey of the previous decade in art and art education, summarized in its title the feeling of most of those close to the arts.

Before World War I serious music in the United States was almost entirely derivative, an undistinguished imitation of European forms. Americans might do the composing but the result was German, French, or Italian music. Respectability in this art form was inextricably bound to Old World standards. Attempts to be original were taken by the prewar musical establishment to be signs of deficient taste. On the eve of the twenties the nation's most accomplished and fresh-thinking composer, Charles Ives, had to make his living selling insurance. Returning at the end of his business day to a farm in Connecticut, Ives used the midnight hours to write music no one cared to hear.

The postwar decade, however, brought a change to American music. Fresh winds swept the field, new names appeared, and the quality of the nation's musical life advanced on all fronts. In the 1920s alone some fifty major orchestras arose in the United States. Community and school orchestras, even esoteric groups such as string quartets, increased proportionately. Good music became available to Americans living in the cultural hinterlands as well as in the cities. The advent of radio broadcasting helped the dissemination significantly. The National Broadcasting Company, organized in 1926, featured "great" music in its inaugural program and went on in the same year to sponsor twenty weekly symphonic broadcasts directed by Walter Damrosch. The combined audience for the series was estimated at two hundred million people. In 1927 American radio carried its first opera as well as the Boston Symphony Orchestra and New York Philharmonic Orchestra in concert. Two years later the Philharmonic began its regular Sunday afternoon broadcasts, and an American cultural institution was born. Some conductors, of course, were skeptical of the new media, but most agreed with Damrosch that with the assistance of the airwaves they could reach more people with one performance than they did in five years of concert work. Music education also thrived in the milieu of the twenties. The Eastman School of Music (1921) at the University of Rochester, the Juilliard School (1923) in New York, and the Curtis Institute (1924) in Philadelphia quickly became the nerve centers of American music. Their programs, according to R. L. Duffus in 1928, "are working to raise the standard of America's musical competence and taste." But there was a further goal. "It is ... their deliberate purpose," Duffus declared, "to flavor the teaching and making of music in America with the salt of originality. They are striving to give us a voice of our own, which shall not be merely an overtone of Europe."

Original American music benefited greatly from the advent of bold organizations expressly designed to offer it assistance: Pro Musica (1920), the International Composers' Guild in New York (1921), and the League of Composers (1923). Pro Musica was devoted to propagandizing for modern music. *New Music*, a quarterly begun in California by pioneer composer Henry Cowell, published full scores of American compositions. The friendship of important conductors was also essential, and two of the best in the twenties, Leopold Stokowski and Serge Koussevitzky, agreed to play the new, native music. Even the jazz idiom, incorporated in serious compositions, found its way into the nation's most august concert halls. "By the end of the twenties," composer Aaron Copland declared, "music that was greeted with snickers and sarcasm . . . won its place in the sun. . . . The decade 1920–1930 definitely marks the influx of new music in the U.S.A."

Copland himself did much to bring this about. His birth in 1900 in a drab section of Brooklyn to a nonmusical family did not auger well for a musical career. But on his own initiative Copland secured basic instruction. At first he studied traditional harmony, rhythm, and construction with their regularities and rules. But gradually he became attracted to modern, freer forms of musical expression. Advanced training in these techniques, however, was nonexistent in America, and so in 1921 Copland jumped at the chance to study in Paris. He remained three years, working under the tutelage of Nadia Boulanger and delighting in the heady atmosphere of musical innovation in postwar France. There was no resemblance whatsoever between Copland and the stereotype of the American expatriate sitting alienated and disillusioned in a Paris bar. In fact Copland in Europe remained anxious to return to his native land and apply his talents to the task of revolutionizing its music. The United States, as he put it, was "virgin soil" for musical pioneering.

In 1924, when Copland returned to America, it was not easy to enter the musical establishment. Despite his ideals and abilities Copland had to content himself with making a living as a pianist on the summer hotel circuit. Yet soon he made contact with sympathetic people at the League of Composers, and, through the League's good offices, two of his radical piano pieces were performed late in 1924 in New York. The following January the New York Symphony Orchestra staged Copland's *Symphony for Organ and Orchestra* with Walter Damrosch as conductor and Nadia Boulanger herself as soloist. The performance stunned conservatives, and at its conclusion Damrosch, tongue in cheek, turned to the audience and remarked that "if a young man at the age of twenty-three can write a symphony like that, in five years he will be ready to commit murder." Copland, however, was elated just because his music was performed. Further encouragement came quickly from Serge Koussevitzky, the new conductor of the Boston Symphony, who promised to play his scores. Copland later recalled that he was then ready "to write a work that would immediately be recognized as American in character." The *Symphony,* in his opinion, was still under too much European influence.

With the assistance of a 1925 Guggenheim Fellowship, the first awarded to a composer, Copland began experimenting with the complex, clashing polyrhythms of jazz in an effort to put them to use in symphonic compositions. The results, *Music for the Theatre* (1925) and *Piano Concerto* (1926), established Copland as a major innovator. At the conclusion of the twenties Copland won a national competition with *Dance Symphony* and prepared to move on to scores that were distinctively American in sound as well as name: *Billy the Kid, Rodeo,* and *Appalachian Spring.*

Brooklyn, New York also produced another young composer who adorned the twenties: George Gershwin. The performance of his *Rhapsody in Blue* on February 12, 1924, in New York's Aeolian Hall by Paul Whiteman's orchestra was a landmark in the history of American music. The house was packed for what Whiteman billed as an "Experiment in Modern Music," and word flashed out that a new musical genius had been discovered. Explaining his esthetic inspiration for the piece in a 1928 interview, Gershwin confessed: "the vivid panorama of American life swept through my mind—its feverishness, its vulgarity, its welter of love, marriage, divorce, and its basic solidarity in the character of the American people. All the emotional reactions excited by contemplating the American scene were stuffed into the first outline of the Rhapsody."

Before conducting Gershwin's next composition, *Concerto in F* (1925), Walter Damrosch, still facile with impromptu curtain speeches, told the audience that Gershwin was "the Prince who has taken Cinderella [jazz] by the hand and openly proclaimed her a princess to the astonished world, no doubt to the fury of her envious sisters." Speaking of his own art, Gershwin remarked, "jazz I regard as an American folk-music...I believe that it can be made the basis of serious symphonic works of lasting value in the hands of a composer with a talent for both jazz and symphonic music." Gershwin, of course, was the man and the result was symphonic jazz. Using this blend of old and new musical forms to express the contemporary scene, Gershwin wrote the rhapsodic ballet *An American in Paris* in 1928. Rave reviews greeted its initial performance in Carnegie Hall. The unmistakably American *Porgy and Bess* followed in 1935, two years before Gershwin's untimely death.

Jazz, Gershwin consistently maintained, was America's only native music. "When jazz is played in another nation, it is called American. When it is played in another country, it sounds false. Jazz is the result of the energy stored up in America . . . jazz has contributed an enduring value to America in the sense that it has expressed ourselves. It is an original American achievement." It followed that the serious composer in search of a distinctive national style would do well to consider the uses of jazz. Copland and Gershwin had shown the way with their symphonic or orchestrated jazz. Pure jazz, however, was unwritten, improvised, and unrehearsed—a performers' rather than a composers' art. There were those who disparaged it as a nonart, a product of brothels and savage minds, but for its devotees jazz became not only an art but a virtual religion. The new music came from New Orleans to Chicago, St. Louis, and, early in 1917, New York City with the Original Dixieland Jazz Band. Within three years the jazz craze was nationwide. Those who wished to transcend accepted standards of form and taste found jazz to their liking. It was an antidote to conformity, boredom, custom, tradition. Its beat both soothed and excited. It was the perfect sound for a nervous generation. And while spontaneously creating jazz, American musicians were finally satisfying the chronic demand for cultural distinctiveness.

Music in the 1920s in America included so much fresh talent that the time indeed seemed one of renaissance or, it could really be said, of *first* birth. Roger Sessions, Howard Hanson, Walter Piston, Henry Cowell, and Roy Harris began composing during the decade. The last two, from California and Oklahoma respectively, were especially committed to the idea that great American music had to reflect the American national character. This necessitated the composer's being in close contact with grass roots sounds and subjects. Frederick Converse certainly was in his *Flivver 10,000,000 . . . Fantasy for Orchestra Inspired by the Famous Legend "The Ten Millionth Ford Is Now Serving Its Owner"* which the Boston Symphony performed in 1927. The titles of Ferde Grofé compositions, *Broadway at Night* (1924) and *Mississippi Suite* (1925), also suggest that the source of his inspiration was native. The *Grand Canyon Suite* was completed just after the end of the twenties. John Alden Carpenter's *Krazy Kat* was based on a newspaper cartoon character. George

Antheil utilized airplane engines, doorbells, and typewriters to put his conception of American reality into music.

Older composers, active before the war, also flourished in the cultural explosion of the twenties. Among them Daniel Gregory Mason was self-confessedly conservative with a preference for classical forms and themes. But even Mason was not oblivious to the surge of musical nationalism. His *String Quartet on Negro Themes* appeared in 1919 and nine years later came *Chanticleer Overture*, a score inspired by Mason's reading of Henry David Thoreau and written to catch "the American Spirit." Ernest Bloch, an older Swedish-American, likewise became a fervent musical nationalist in the twenties. Indeed his *America* of 1927 was an attempt to express the meaning and destiny of the United States and was dedicated to Lincoln and Whitman. Charles Ives also chose historical themes in his *Concord Sonata* (1920), which contained movements named after Emerson, Hawthorne, the Alcotts, and Thoreau. Ives also experimented with a flexible score, giving the conductor the option of selecting one of several variations of a passage. The willingness of American composers to break tradition in this manner and to utilize their own past instead of Europe's for inspiration were the most significant developments in music in the twenties.

One musical genre in which American composers seemed particularly adept after the war was the musical play or comedy. The twenties were alive with great names—Jerome Kern, Cole Porter, Irving Berlin, Richard Rodgers, Lorenz Hart. The songs they wrote proved to be both popular and lasting. Perhaps the preeminent musical of the time was Kern and Hammerstein's *Showboat* of 1927 which does not hesitate to treat delicate racial and sexual problems.

The change in attitude of Deems Taylor is representative of what the 1920s did for American music. Shortly after the war, Taylor, a composer, joined Harold Stearns' group of intellectuals in writing a book-length critique entitled *Civilization in the United States*. Taylor's essay on music lamented that, in spite of the nation's great orchestras and opera houses, "there has never been a successful opera by an American offered at [an] opera house, and the number of viable American orchestral works is small enough to be counted almost upon one's fingers. We squander millions every year upon an art we cannot produce." By the end of the twenties such a dour portrait was no longer valid. American works were being written, staged, and appreciated. In 1927, in fact, the Metropolitan Opera

House produced its first American opera, *The King's Henchmen,* which was received with widespread enthusiasm. Its composer was Deems Taylor.

American painting, like American music, stood in the shadow of Europe as the 1920s began. Even the modernists experimented according to Old World formulas as the 1913 Armory Show and its aftermath attested. But style made little difference; Americans were generally unsympathetic to any kind of art. The resulting poverty for the painter cast a pall of gloom over the art world. Conditions, however, brightened measurably during the decade. There had, for instance, been no institutional support for modern art in 1920, but by the end of the twenties the Museum of Modern Art, the Pennsylvania Academy of Fine Art, and the Whitney Museum exhibited and patronized radical native artists. The Art Students League helped ward off the disparagements of antimodernist critics. Galleries were also increasingly willing to show and collectors to buy nonrepresentational art. The public no longer expected paintings to look like photographs. Canvasses that depicted the artist's inner emotional state (or that which he wanted to create in the viewer), rather than nature, gained favor. Deliberately distorting reality, the modernists strove for greater esthetic freedom. As their painting created wider circles of appreciation, American art gained new vitality.

Among the nonrepresentational painters in the twenties, Charles Demuth, Charles Sheeler, Joseph Stella, and Niles Spencer can be grouped together as practitioners of the cubist tradition. They shared a tendency to reduce scenes to their basic structural elements like cubes and squares. Demuth began to paint architectural motifs in 1919 and soon developed a flat, perspectiveless style. His *Modern Conveniences* of 1921, for example, resembles an architect's blueprint, with unrelated lines slanting across a two-story building. Sheeler, on the other hand, stressed depth and perspective. *Church Street El,* a New York scene painted in 1920, is so sharply shadowed as to give the appearance of a totally abstract composition. Only at second glance can the viewer distinguish the cubes and lines of skyscrapers, tracks, and trains. Sheeler also found beauty in the industrial landscape, and he painted a series of canvasses of Henry Ford's huge River Rouge plant near Detroit. One of Sheeler's most powerful works is a 1922 study of yachts running before the wind—a straining, curving pattern of triangles. In the art of Joseph Stella, an Italian immigrant, the geometric forms of city scenes expressed the speed, power, and greatness of modern America. New York's Brooklyn Bridge, painted in a number of variations over several years, was Stella's favorite subject. His most striking renditions emphasize the bridge cables sweeping upward in a gesture of deification to the city skyline beyond. In a five-panel composition, *New York Interpreted* (1922), Stella endeavors to catch the exhilarating qualities of the nation's largest city. On the extremes of cubism, Spencer reduced reality to a geometry of blocks and cylinders. Instead of being alienated from urban-industrial America of the 1920s, such painters used it as the basis of a new esthetic.

Other practitioners of modern art in the twenties ranged far afield for subject matter. Georgia O'Keeffe revolted against the photographic tradition of American landscape painting to interpret the western deserts with expressionist techniques. She also painted *Black Spot*—which was simply that! O'Keeffe's *The American Radiator Building* (1929), with its windows glowing in the night sky, is more literal, and received critical acclaim as a major statement of American expressionism. Stuart Davis went to the extremes of abstractionism with *Egg Beater No. 1* and *Boats, Gloucester* which hardly correspond to their titles. Another radical, Arthur Dove, pioneered in the 1920s with collages, achieving surrealistic effects.

John Marin's multifaceted talent was one of the brightest of the twenties. His preferred medium, water color, lent itself nicely to subjects as diverse as the Maine coast and the Manhattan skyline. A passionate, exhuberant man, Marin's esthetic ideal was the communication of his emotions and, ultimately, the articulation of the spirit of America. Because he painted his moods, not external reality, Marin tapped an inexhaustible source of artistic inspiration. In 1928 he staged the twenty-first one-man show of his career. By this time he was established as the ablest water colorist in American art, and modern art itself was an accepted part of American culture. Only the most stolid critics refused to recognize the new movement's esthetic potential.

In spite of their dominant position in the twenties, the modernists faced a strong challenge from those who continued in the realist tradition. George Bellows, John Sloan, and George Luks, all members of the prewar Ash Can School of painting that depicted the seamy side of city life, produced outstanding representational canvasses in the twenties. Joining them were newer realists like Edward

Hopper, Charles Burchfield, and Morris Kantor who eagerly sought beauty in coal mines, factories, and skid rows. Some painters, like Walt Kuhn, a force behind the Armory Show, returned to the fold of realism in the twenties after flirting with more radical styles.

Nationalism, or more correctly, regionalism, motivated a number of artists to turn for subject matter to everyday American people and scenes. Such realistic, local color painting was not begun by the New Deal's Works Project Administration, as widely supposed, but actually started in 1928 with John Stuart Curry's *Baptism in Kansas*. Before the decade was over Curry added several other major works delineating the trials and tribulations of the rural Midwest and South. Another practitioner of this genre, Thomas Hart Benton, was a descendant of the Missouri senator of the same name. Benton deliberately revolted against the modernistic revolutionaires as well as against European influence in order to paint the common life of common people in the Missouri valley with nationalistic fervor. Grant Wood, the third important regionalist, also began his work in the late 1920s. Wood's sympathetic and realistic portrayal of a staid, pious, farm couple in *American Gothic* (1930) is the best possible answer to the stereotype of the roaring twenties as it is to the myth of a dissipated and alienated generation of American intellectuals.

American sculpture in the postwar decade was distinguished by the heavy, distorted nudes of French-born Gaston Lachaise who adopted the United States as his home because, in his opinion, "the soil most fertile for the continuity of art—is here." The chisels of William Zorach, Arnold Bonnebeck, and Robert Garrison, among others, brought expressionism to sculpture, while Jo Davidson, the "head hunter," and Paul Manship continued to carve realistically. Of dubious artistic merit, but ardently American in theme and size, were Gutzon Borglum's busts carved into the sides of mountains in Georgia and South Dakota. His Atlanta monument celebrated Confederate heroes; the carvings in South Dakota, Presidents Washington, Jefferson, Lincoln, and Theodore Roosevelt.

The twenties were not exceptionally creative or nationalistic in architecture. Louis Sullivan, the pioneer functionalist, died penniless and unrecognized in a run-down Chicago rooming house in 1924. His pupil Frank Lloyd Wright, who had enjoyed limited success before World War I, found himself unemployed. The major commissions and applause went to practitioners of classical, Gothic, and colonial styles of building. At Yale University James Gamble Rogers built imitation medieval buildings complete with windowpanes deliberately broken and then repaired in the medieval manner. Beautiful as it was, the Lincoln Memorial (dedicated in 1922) was more appropriate for Pericles than the man it sought to honor. In Chicago architects John Howells and Raymond Hood decorated the skyscraping Tribune Tower (1925) with pseudo-Gothic ornamentation and flying buttresses in total disregard of functionalist esthetics.

Still there were some encouraging harbingers. In second place behind Howells and Hood in the *Tribune* competition of 1922 was Eliel Saarinen whose entry delighted the functionalists and modernists. Shortly thereafter Saarinen left his native Finland to join the faculty of the University of Michigan, design world-famous lake and river fronts for Chicago and Detroit, and draw plans for the striking Cranbrook School near Detroit. The skyscraper, too, seemed about to realize its full esthetic potential. According to one observer of the *Tribune* competition, "we are about to bid a glad farewell to the standard formula for the skyscraper design, with its Graeco-Roman or Byzantine feet, its geometrically punctured torso, and its Renaissance topgear." Certainly New York City's Empire State Building, designed by Shreve, Lamb, and Harmon between 1928 and 1931, was a step away from the norm. The clean, undecorated simplicity of its lines pointed toward a distinctive and distinguished American style.

In residential design Frank Lloyd Wright kept the spark of his genius alive in the twenties with a few commissions in California. His esthetic ideals were also advanced by several young Europeans like Raymond Schindler, William Lescaze, and Richard Neutra, all of whom immigrated to this country between 1914 and 1923. Daring to use new materials and forms, and basing their designs on human needs and tastes rather than on traditional formulas, Wright and his followers blew fresh wind over the entire architectural endeavor.

The flowering of the literary arts in the 1920s is indisputable and well documented. American poets, playwrights, and novelists flourished in the heady atmosphere of esthetic freedom provided by the erosion of the old standards. The time seemed ripe for experimentation—in form, in content, in purpose. Edna Ferber, the best-selling novelist, expressed the impatience creative minds shared. Writing in the *Bookman* in 1920 she implored America to "stop being ashamed of its art." "It's time we stopped imitating," she continued; "let's write in the American fashion about America. . . . We've got color, and romance, and glow, and vivacity, and depth all the way from Maine to Manila."

American theater came of age in the postwar years. The tyranny of the romantic comedy with its invariably happy ending, of the bedroom farce, and of the mystery was broken. Playwrights either moved toward a new sort of realism or pioneered with freer, expressionist techniques. Among the realists, Maxwell Anderson and Laurence Stallings stood out with *What Price Glory?*, first produced in New York on September 3, 1924. The play's opening line contains a four-letter word, as does its concluding line, and in between the unsavory reality of men at war is laid bare. The preeminent expressionist of the twenties, Eugene O'Neill, is a strong contender for the most talented American dramatist of any era. He came directly to grips with the tragedy of human existence. "Our lives," says Nina Leeds in *Strange Interlude* (1928), "are merely strange dark interludes [where] . . . the soul is scraped clean of impure flesh and made worthy to bleach in peace." Seeking only to portray his conception of the human situation, O'Neill discarded the established conventions of the theater. He experimented successfully with Freudian psychology (see page 54). Intricate symbolism, masks, and asides to the audience succeeded in revealing the inner emotions of his characters with striking effectiveness. In *Dynamo* (1929) O'Neill created a powerful study in self-deception. The protagonist, Reuben Light, renounces religion and turns instead to worshipping the dynamo at a power plant where he is employed. His devotion to the machine and science leads him into inhuman acts. In the final scene Reuben asks the dynamo for love, but the whirring black idol does not respond. Reuben then throws himself upon it and is immolated. Such portrayals of disillusion and despair were O'Neill's stock in trade. Yet as an artist he personally avoided their grasp. O'Neill used despair to create great theater. The theme of disillusion proved rich in artistic potential.

O'Neill's talent did not go unrecognized in the twenties. The Provincetown Players, a group that spearheaded the new theater, first produced his plays. He went on to win an enthusiastic following with *Anna Christy* (1921), *The Hairy Ape* (1922), *Desire under the Elms* (1925), and *Strange Interlude* (1928). The last ran for more than four hundred performances on Broadway and then toured the country. *Strange Interlude*, moreover, required five and one-half hours to perform (O'Neill intended that the audience eat supper during a long intermission). Another radical group, the Theatre Guild, supported O'Neill in the 1920s. His work fitted the Guild's aim of making available drama of artistic merit and adult content regardless of profit considerations.

The burgeoning motion-picture industry of the twenties, however, was notoriously profit conscious and generally took the lowest common denominator as its esthetic criterion. Much of Hollywood's production in the decade was hardly art. Still a few imaginative writers and directors began to explore the possibilities of the silent (until 1928) film as a new artistic medium. Thomas Ince, Maurice Tourneur, and Cecil B. DeMille extended the technical refinements initiated by the great prewar producer David Wark Griffith. Mack Sennett, a protégé of Griffith, specialized in the creation of slapstick comedies, and in 1915 launched the pantomimist Charles Chaplin on a meteoric career that led to the top of the acting profession in the twenties. Another Griffith colleague, Austrian-born Erich von Stroheim, brought an uncompromising realism to the American screen. In Robert Flaherty American film had a masterful photographer-writer-director of striking originality. His *Nanook of the North* (1922) was the first successful feature-length documentary. But Hollywood, hungry for the melodramatic romance, turned its back on his beautiful and authentic *Moana* (1926), a study of Samoan life and philosophy. *The Cabinet of Dr. Caligari,* produced in Germany and brought to the United States in 1921, was the most artistically significant film of the decade. Deliberately distorted, *Caligari* endeavors to present reality as seen through the eyes of a madman. American artists and intellectuals, previously indifferent to motion pictures, greeted it with enthusiasm as a contribution to expressionist techniques. A few Americans attempted to follow *Caligari's* lead in using the full range of communication available in cinema. The results, still slender in the twenties, included films such as *Human Wreckage,* which purports to show the world as it appears to a drug addict.

In 1928 Harriet Monroe's *Poetry: A Magazine of Verse* published her observation that "during the last few years there has been a remarkable renascence of poetry in both America and England, and an equally extraordinary revival of public interest in the art." *Poetry* itself, one of a number of avant garde magazines begun in the five years preceding American intervention in World War I, contributed significantly to the revival. The new poems it published attempted, in Monroe's words, to achieve "absolute simplicity and sincerity." Their beauty stemmed from their ability to present "a concrete and immediate realization of life." A number of American poets worked according to this creed in the 1920s. Some, like Ezra Pound and T. S. Eliot, had been active before the war, innovating with verse form and diction in an effort to articulate their ideas. They continued to write in the twenties and were joined by newer rebels like e e cummings (who disdained conventional punctuation), Wallace Stevens, Conrad Aiken, Robinson Jeffers, and Hart Crane. Women contributed too, with Edna St. Vincent Millay and Marianne Moore heading the list. Robert Frost continued to write deceptively simple poems with New England settings.

As for the American novel in the 1920s, it is only necessary to note that Ernest Hemingway, Sinclair Lewis, Thomas Wolfe, F. Scott Fitzgerald, John Dos Passos, Sherwood Anderson, and William Faulkner all published their first major works in the decade to distinguish it as one of exceptional richness. Moreover, able older novelists like Willa Cather, Theodore Dreiser, Ellen Glasgow, and Edith Wharton were still active. In the novel of the twenties virtually every convention was thrown to the winds. No subject was too delicate to be scrutinized. Contemporary society was ruthlessly dissected. Often the authors turned inward, going to psychology for basic explanations. Gertrude Stein, a nourisher rather than a creator of significant fiction, molded words, syntax, and the rhythm of sentences in an effort to convey meaning. One of her star pupils, Ernest Hemingway, developed a highly effective style featuring taut, stripped sentences, understatement, and a dearth of adjectives.

Novelists as well as poets, artists, and musicians contributed to the multifaceted cultural explosion of black America in the postwar period. "On a bright September morning in 1921," recalled poet Langston Hughes, "I came up out of the subway at 135th and Lenox into the beginnings of the Negro Renaissance." Also known as the Harlem Renaissance (it centered in New York City's black ghetto of that name), the phenomenon represented the identification by black artists and intellectuals of their racial heritage and its exploitation for cultural purposes. Hughes himself contributed *The Weary Blues* (1926)—a collection of poems—and a novel, *Not Without Laughter* (1930). Joining him in the cultural sunshine of the 1920s were older black writers of distinction such as Claude McKay and James Weldon Johnson. The poems in *Harlem Shadows* (1922) and *Home to Harlem* (1928), a novel of black life in New York, placed McKay at the forefront of the renaissance. In addition to writing poetry, Johnson collected, edited, and published black spirituals and sermons. These efforts furthered the quest for the recovery of the black identity that Carter G. Woodson's Association for the Study of Negro Life and History had launched in 1915. Among the younger black intellectuals, in addition to Hughes, Jean Toomer and Countee Cullen stood out. The former's *Cane* (1923), a combination of prose and poetry, ranks with the best American literary production of the decade. Cullen published *Color* in 1925 when he was only twenty-two years old. His poems, like most of the writing of the Harlem Renaissance, were focused on the black man's unhappy situation in American society, but they also had an esthetic significance that transcended the protest purpose.

The new literary outpouring of blacks found an audience in the pages of periodicals like *Crisis* and *Opportunity*. White Americans learned about the renaissance in *Survey Graphic's* special Harlem issue edited by Alain Locke, a Harvard Ph.D. and the first black Rhodes scholar. While literature dominated the movement, Aaron Douglass did creditable drawings and black theater flourished. Music was the basis for a major part of the creative effort of the decade. Both as a practitioner and composer of jazz, Duke Ellington became a symbol of this new art form, the appeal of which easily crossed the color line.

There was nothing lost about a generation of creative intellectuals like those who shaped American culture in the 1920s. Release from the esthetic canons of the past stimulated a creative outpouring that was remarkable both in quantity and quality. Beneath the ballyhoo and the affected despair lay immense energy and optimism in regard to the arts. World War I shocked and dismayed but it also liberated. Artists discovered the esthetic possibilities of being lost. In some cases they *used* the war and its disillusion to fashion great art. To be sure, the American artist-intellectual stood quite apart from the vast majority of his contemporaries. There was, however, a distinct esthetic advantage in not having to produce for public approval. Capitalizing on the unique opportunities of the postwar years, American artists produced a record with which few decades in the national experience can compare.

Ethics

Examination of a period's formal discussion of ethics (values, morals, or standards might also be used) offers a revealing approach to its intellectual life. Ethics in this sense, of course, means something other than what does, or does not, happen in the back seats of automobiles. It relates, rather, to moral philosophy—to man's search for the solid foundations of right and wrong, good and bad, on which belief can be anchored. Intellectuals have traditionally made this exploration their special concern. In the 1920s the debate over values was especially energetic. Some Americans clung determinedly to the old absolutes. But the clamor of dissatisfaction rang through the period. Many regarded belief in the absolute as lazy, a substitute for creative thinking. For others it was an outright lie, undermined by the new science and the need for social adjustments. But as the old standards fell the incentive to create new ones increased. Few intellectuals of the twenties lapsed into the nihilism and despair so often attributed to the postwar years.

The Humanists (or New Humanists) of the 1920s were not numerous, but their presence demonstrates that old ethics could at least survive in the new era. For these intellectuals control, balance, and order were the cardinal virtues. Adherence to a strict moral code was necessary to attain them. The Humanists believed that fundamental law underlay morality. The law consisted of a set of ethical and esthetic norms inherent in, but always above, nature, and articulated by the world's great religions, literature, and art. It followed that right and wrong were constants—absolutes that did not change with changing circumstances but persisted through the ages. The best that man could do, according to the Humanists, was to follow these unvarying values. And, fortunately, man possessed both reason and a moral sense or will that enabled him to intuit the ethical absolutes and use them to restrain his lower nature. In this way order and decorum were secured, beauty created, and progress achieved.

Humanism was an expression of what George Santayana labeled in 1911 "the genteel tradition." It drew heavily, according to Henry May's *End of American Innocence*, on the "nineteenth century credo": a composite belief in the reality, certainty, and eternity of moral values, in the possibility of progress, and in the beneficence of traditional Anglo-Saxon culture. The Humanists were philosophical idealists. They felt they knew how people ought to behave, and they endeavored to bring thought and conduct up to the ideal type. Understandably, they considered quality more important than quantity. And they stressed the importance for the individual of cultivating the inner man and rising above the mediocrity of the mass.

Humanism had several prominent spokesmen in the 1920s. Irving Babbitt, a Harvard professor, and Paul Elmer More of Princeton and the *Nation* championed the position before, during, and after World War I. Both were Middle Westerners, Harvard graduates, classicists, and philosophers. Both criticized the tendency of romanticism, naturalism, and pragmatism to break down ethical and esthetic absolutes.

"The real question," according to More in 1928, "is not whether there are standards, but whether they shall be based on tradition or struck out brand new by each individual critic." Casting his vote with the first option, More praised the thinker or artist who discerned permanent values and thereby enabled man to raise himself from bestiality to his higher, divine nature. In More's opinion the relativists who rejected such values were both indolent and conceited; they followed the easy way of their own fancies. Mental and moral discipline demanded sustained effort, but success in curbing the lower appetites was the highest pinnacle of human achievement.

Babbitt (who must have rued the coincidence of his name with that of Sinclair Lewis' famous character) joined More in praise of order. He especially admired the American Puritans who were able to place an inner check on man's natural impulses. In fact the problem with modern America, in Babbitt's estimation, was a preoccupation with material progress at the expense of moral progress. There was a dearth of standards and restraints. Responsibility—to anything higher than oneself—had melted under the force of the relativists' sun. "The American reading his Sunday paper in a state of lazy collapse," Babbitt complained, "is perhaps the most perfect symbol of the triumph of quantity over quality that the world has yet seen." But equally deplorable were satirists and literary critics like Henry L. Mencken, Harold Stearns, Van Wyck Brooks, and Randolph Bourne, who, according to Babbitt, struck down the very standards intellectuals had a special responsibility to uphold.

A Harvard protégé of Babbitt and an admirer of More, Stuart P. Sherman lent his remarkable energies to the Humanist cause after World War I. Bourne, disparagingly, branded him "the last brave offshoot of the genteel tradition." His first book, on Matthew Arnold, appeared in 1917, and before his untimely death nine years later Sherman wrote ten more. Taken together they underscored the need for certainties and absolutes. Following the Humanist tradition, Sherman sought such bedrock in the past, and he singled out the American past, in preference to that of Greece and Rome, for special praise. He berated the young intellectuals of the twenties who disdained the American heritage. Their work lacked optimism and moral vigor, in his opinion, because they turned their backs on the values inherent in their own culture. Emerson, with his strong belief in spiritual truth and moral law, especially appealed to Sherman. The Puritans were attractive for the same reason. Sherman had no patience with intellectuals who "make their 'truth' as they need it." He refused, therefore, to accept the pragmatic definition of goodness. Under the guise of romanticism, intellectuals had too long followed their individual criteria. "We have trusted our instincts," Sherman declared in 1917, "long enough to sound the depths of their treacherousness. We have followed nature to the last ditch and ditch water." And under the guise of science, men mistakenly assumed that "the laws of the physical universe [suffice for] the moral requirements of man." With the assumed blessings of naturalism, the educator observed dogs and drew conclusions for training children and the novelist returned from the zoo with a wish to "revise the relations of the sexes so as to satisfy the average man's natural craving for three wives." In Sherman's creed man should stand apart from the natural world. "The great revolutionary task of the nineteenth-century thinkers," he said on one occasion, "was to put man into nature. The great task of twentieth-century thinkers is to get him out again." Only by disciplining the natural man with moral laws and stable values could tooth and claw existence be transcended and the world achieve "order, stability, justice, gentleness, and wisdom." As proof of his point, Sherman offered World War I.

The Humanists were not consistently religious in spite of the fact that they eschewed naturalism. Yet many who joined them in defending traditional values in the 1920s held strong religious convictions. Indeed T. S. Eliot warned the Humanists, Norman Foerster in particular, that "you must either be a naturalist or a supernaturalist." If you did not believe that ethics came from biological necessity and social circumstance, you *had* to attribute them to a supernatural agency. As Eliot saw it, the only basis for regarding man apart from nature, as the Humanists did, was man's link with the supernatural.

Eliot himself was openly religious. *The Waste Land* of 1922 argued for the importance of values and for a sense of the past, and for belief in a realm higher than the material. It was necessary to accept on faith even that which science could not prove. A rock of unalterable law was essential, from Eliot's standpoint, to the intellectual welfare of humanity in the modern age. The trouble with the people in *The Waste Land* is that they had lost this capacity to believe. Eliot himself turned to Anglo-Catholicism in the mid-1920s. Faith was vital, he declared in 1931, to "renew and rebuild civilization and save the World from Suicide."

The genteel tradition also found expression in novels during the 1920s. Willa Cather praised the driving, guiding, sustaining force of religious belief in *Death Comes for the Archbishop* (1927). In this work the faith of the Spanish padres in the Southwest proves sufficiently strong to overcome both naturalism and negativism. *Shadows on the Rock* (1931) is likewise an assertion of the importance of belief and of the value of the past. The writing in the twenties of Thornton Wilder, Booth Tarkington, and Ellen Glasgow also defended morality and integrity. Edith Wharton's *The Age of Innocence* (1920) attacks conventional morality but ultimately accepts it as indispensable for ordered existence. Refusing to regard World War I as a watershed, such thinkers kept the traditional values of Western culture alive in the twenties.

Despite the strength of its proponents' convictions, Humanism encountered vigorous and persistent dissent in the 1920s. Its chief opponents, the Modernists, discounted the old certainties and rejected absolutes. The dialogue between these two positions provided one of the major intellectual themes of the decade. While the discussion frequently concerned the merits of contemporary literature, the real issue at stake was the nature of value.

There were salvos between Babbitt and More on the one side and Bourne and Mencken, for example, on the other for a number of years, but the controversy reached a crescendo in 1928, 1929, and 1930. Virtually every intellectual became involved, at least to the extent of having opinions. The weapons used were usually reviews and essays in literary periodicals, but in 1930 two book-length works expounded the conflicting viewpoints. The Humanist manifesto was *Humanism and America: Essays on the Outlook of Modern Civiliza-*

tion, edited by Norman Foerster. In his preface to the collection Foerster opened fire on the Modernists who "made of revolt and scepticism ends rather than beginnings of wisdom." These iconoclasts, according to Foerster, were symptoms of, not remedies for, the sorry condition of American civilization. But Foerster took heart from his conviction that the nation's intellectual climate was swinging back to an appreciation of permanent values. "More and more persons, oppressed with the stale scepticism of the post-war period, are beginning to grow sceptical of that scepticism, and are looking for a new set of controlling ideas capable of restoring value to human existence." Humanism was one force making for order. Foerster defined it, broadly, as "a belief that the proper study of mankind is man, and that this study should enable mankind to perceive and realise its humanity." Such study showed, in Foerster's estimation, that man lived on three planes—the natural, the human, and the religious. It was the Humanists' task to disengage the human level from either extreme. Man must be neither animal nor God. This required the "peculiarly human" power of restraint. Foerster called upon man to extract spiritual truth and ethical norms from the supernatural world and use these values to check the lower, natural instincts. The result was an ideal humanness and the good life.

Foerster turned next to a defense of the Humanists from charges of being academic, un-American, reactionary, and Puritan. His technique was not to deny these postures but rather to redefine them, giving them favorable connotations. "Academic" became, to Foerster, an interest in knowledge. "Un-American" meant simply a respect for the triumphs of foreign cultures and a desire to fuse them into the native strain. Similarly, admiration of the past could be a real cultural asset. The Renaissance, he pointed out, was a revival of ancient learning and, thus, reactionary. As for the charge of being Puritanical, Foerster welcomed it, taking it to mean the possession of faith and the ability to use that faith for the achievement of order and discipline. The twentieth-century critics of the Puritans, in his view, were "those who throw down the reins [and] are simply abandoning their humanity to the course of animal life or the complacency of vegetables."

The principal reply to Foerster and his colleagues was *The Critique of Humanism: A Symposium,* edited by C. Hartley Grattan. Grattan was only twenty-eight at the time of its publication, and he did not bother to disguise his impatience with an old-fashioned doctrine that was, in his view, inconsistent with reality, stifling to creativity, and opposed to progress. Grattan's own contribution to the symposium came squarely to grips with the question of value. He began by rejecting the Humanist notion of the separateness of man and nature. There were no lower and higher levels of experience. Grattan consequently rejected the idea of value as emanating from a higher reality. Man, in a word, was natural. The human mind was an organ, like the heart or liver, and had no power to intuit higher truth. Indeed, there was no reason for even positing the existence of such truth in Grattan's estimation. What the Humanists really did, he continued, was to derive values from past literature and a vague "wisdom of the ages." But since man in the past had the same limitations as present man, the whole Humanist structure collapsed in shambles. In Grattan's estimation Humanism boiled down to unfounded and indefensible dogma.

Turning to his own Modernist understanding of value, Grattan made clear at the outset that "our quarrel is not with values as such." Standards and ethics were necessary to civilized living. The crux of the issue was not the desirability but the source of values. Grattan believed that the only certain values came from science. He believed that man was part of nature and should be studied with the same methods as, say, a plant or mineral. Values would be ascertained by allegedly objective experimentation. A pragmatic criterion should apply: if adhering to a certain value system advanced the quest for the good life, then that system would be accepted. Evidence to the contrary, however, would prompt a reformulation of ethics. There were no absolutes. "The remedy for the present situation," Grattan concluded, "is not less science but more science. The extension of the experimental [technique] into the human and social realms is bound to be the most fruitful adventure of modern times."

The other contributors to Grattan's volume were likewise critical of the Humanists. Henry Hazlitt took the absolute-is-lazy position. "Amid the booming, buzzing confusion of new discoveries, doctrines, theories, isms, opinions, it is peaceful, it saves a great deal of anxiety and mental effort, to bow one's head to a traditional authority." Hazlitt, of course, did not approve of this course. *His* anxiety, his nervousness, drove him to experiment with new kinds of authority. For Burton Rascoe, another contributor, the ideas of

Irving Babbitt were "simply those of a Boston Brahmin, holding a university chair, living in academic seclusion from contact with the world of today, happily engaged, like a medieval schoolman, in shadow-boxing with the ghost of Jean-Jacques Rousseau." In Malcolm Cowley's opinion the Modernists were far more influential in "humanizing society" than the Humanists who eschewed current social problems in favor of peering at an allegedly golden past.

The critique of Humanism, it must be stressed, implied no rejection of values as such but only, as Grattan put it, of "the method by which Humanist values are derived." The point is important because the standard treatment of American thought in the 1920s assumes that most intellectuals in these years broke loose from the old norms and drifted in the abyss—the lost generation. In fact the destruction of old values stimulated the construction of new ones.

Reconstruction of values proceeded apace in the nervous generation. Most of those who participated in the rebuilding attempted to establish an ethical system on an empirical, scientific basis. Walter Lippmann's *A Preface to Morals*, published in 1929 after five years of work, is the central statement.

Along with most intellectuals in the twenties (Humanists, of course, excepted) Lippmann recognized the breakdown of belief in external, higher authority as a source of values. Man had been left "in the midst of [a] vast dissolution of ancient habits." The modern generation, Lippmann continued, found it difficult to define right and wrong. The old idea of divine authority had once made morality a matter of discovering the will of God and then conforming to it. There was no "why"; just faith and obedience. Then, gradually, this certainty had been eroded. Science played a major role. So did the modern disinclination to accept *any* arbitrary authority—in government, for instance.

In some quarters it had been supposed that this emancipation would be the key to happiness, but by 1929 Lippmann had his doubts. Man could not exist in a moral vacuum. If civilization was to exist, some ethical system was essential. In *A Preface to Morals* Lippmann nominated his candidate.

The basis of the new morality, Lippmann decided, had to be necessity, common sense, and, most importantly, experience. Taking the pragmatic, relativistic approach, he argued that codes of conduct and social institutions would be evaluated according to how well they worked to produce a satisfactory life. The old codes would not necessarily become passé. Lippmann had no intention of discarding traditional values such as love, honesty, courage, restraint, and unselfishness. Nor did he envisage the replacement of institutions like marriage and the family. These values and social arrangements were practical necessities. They were justified on the basis of human experience and the scientific method of testing observable consequences. Pragmatic criteria led men to act in the manner dictated by religion. God was unnecessary; the same results, in terms of human behavior, could be attained with social science.

In the concluding portion of *A Preface to Morals* Lippmann considered, one by one, the chief values of the world's great religions past and present. In each case he attempted to prove the practicality of the particular law or institution. Writing on the institution of marriage, for example, Lippmann declared: "If it is the truth that the convention of marriage correctly interprets human experience, whereas the separatist conventions [i.e., the practice of separating sex and marriage] are self-defeating, then the convention of marriage will prove to be the conclusion which emerges out of all this immense experimenting. It will survive not as a rule of law imposed by force.... It will not survive as a moral commandment with which the elderly can threaten the young.... It will survive as the dominant insight into the reality of life and happiness, or it will not survive at all." The regulation of sexual behavior through the institution of marriage, then, was a practical matter. The joining of one man and one woman was the product of experiment and experience rather than the whim of an omnipotent deity or a bearded mystic's oracular pronouncement.

The response of the American intellectual community to Lippmann's book provides an insight into the attitude of the 1920s on the subject of value. Most of those who reviewed *A Preface to Morals* accepted as a fact the dissolution of the absolute. Supernaturalism was defunct. But most expressed confidence in modern man's ability to reconstruct morality on a naturalistic basis and applauded Lippmann for his attempt. Edmund Wilson's reaction was typical of the general opinion. Writing in the *New Republic* in July 1929, Wilson agreed with Lippmann that "society left to itself, despite its present bewilderments, may probably be counted upon to evolve a sound morality." *A Preface to Morals*, Wilson continued, was "an antidote to T. S. Eliot ... and to the ... other critics who tend to despair of modern civilization." Lippmann, according to Wilson, gave modern man assurance that even with ancient authorities gone we could "stand on our human feet" in the matter of value.

Other reviewers followed suit. Elmer Davis declared in the *New York Times* that "Mr. Lippmann's title should cheer the pessimist who thinks it is about time to write a postscript to morals." Writing in the *Book-of-the-Month Club News*, Henry Seidel Canby observed that "a moral earthquake" had shaken the Western world since World War I and muddied distinctions between right and wrong. Every thoughtful person, Canby believes, had been searching for a substitute for the "conventional rules that were accepted as final in their youth." Lippmann's book was the answer; it provided a new moral philosophy. In Canby's opinion this made *A Preface to Morals* a book no thoughtful American should miss.

And few, it seemed, did. The book was published in May, 1929, and chosen immediately and unanimously, by five judges, as the Book of the Month. The first printing was 80,000 copies, and there were six more printings before the end of the year. *A Preface to Morals* ranked sixth on the list of best-selling nonfiction for 1929. Lippmann, apparently, spoke reassuring words to an anxious age.

Most intellectual contemporaries of Walter Lippmann shared his impatience with the absolute and the ideal. Indeed thinkers like Oliver Wendell Holmes, Thorstein Veblen, Charles A. Beard, James Harvey Robinson, and John Dewey (others could easily be added) had been participating in what Morton White has called a "revolt against formalism" since the 1880s. The important point about this school of thought for the present purposes is not that it destroyed values in general or revolted from the idea of value, but rather that it sought to create new and better norms. There was no joyous leap into amorality. Those who revolted were highly conscious of the need for values. As moral philosophers they sought to provide a stronger and more relevant ethic than that to which their society subscribed. And World War I did not significantly change their hopes. The intellectual exploration of value continued right through the war years into the twenties.

Of all the varied fields the relativists investigated, none was more important from the standpoint of the philosophy of values than legal theory—the nature of the law. The traditional viewpoint held that written constitutions and statutes reflected a body of eternal truth.

Judges and lawyers endeavored to discern this fundamental, higher law, embody it in the law of the land, and apply it to particular cases. Indeed in the older conception the very possibility of judging was predicated upon the existence of permanent ethical absolutes.

Against this line of thinking first Holmes and then a succession of legal realists aligned themselves. In their opinion the law was, or should be, an empirical science. Instead of using precedent and principle to settle legal questions, the jurist should become a social scientist, observing the consequence of a law and evaluating it according to how well it functioned in solving a human problem. The change was radical. Law, from the new perspective, was made by men and not derived, in Holmes's words, from "a brooding omnipresence in the sky." Man's intelligence, therefore, could be a directive, creative force in life. The essential requirement was that he recognize the experimental, tentative character of norms and values.

Oliver Wendell Holmes's *Collected Legal Papers* stated the legal relativists' position clearly in 1920, but the most influential statement of the decade was Jerome N. Frank's *Law and the Modern Mind*, published in 1930. A great admirer of Holmes, a professional lawyer, and later a judge, Frank insisted upon a functional approach to law. The codes and rules dating back to Hammurabi should be scrapped, in his opinion, as so much dead weight. Not only had changing social conditions made them irrelevant, but they rested on an erroneous notion of higher, permanent truth. The old laws, he contended, were simply "guesses" of earlier generations that had been wrongly made sacrosanct by the passage of time. The scientist had learned to accept truth only on empirical evidence. Why not the lawyer? The reason, Frank thought, was that men, like children, needed a father figure; they craved authority. The import of Frank's book was that if modern men could only summon the courage to let go the father's hand, they could find better forms of authority. In Frank's words, "humanity increases its chances of survival and of progress to the extent that it becomes able to question—neither blindly to accept nor violently to defy—the father's guesses, and to discontinue calling them self-evident truths." The practitioner of jurisprudence, Frank believed, could make a vital contribution to this goal, provided he kept an open mind on the question of value. "The Golden Rule," he declared forthrightly, "is that there is no Golden Rule." But Frank was sceptical, not cynical. He accepted values but "for the time being," as *temporary absolute[s]*." In this way he reconciled the existence of ethics with the freedom to change them.

Frank's redefinition of value did not carry the day among legal philosophers in the 1920s. Traditionalists, like Roscoe Pound and the majority of the justices on the United States Supreme Court, clung to the belief that law had no meaning unless it was grounded on eternal verities. To the older school the Constitution, for instance, was absolute. But joining Frank were a number of vigorous, generally younger, social critics dissatisfied with the effects of adherence to rules long established. Thorstein Veblen, for example, continued into the twenties his sweeping assault on unbending American ethics. Changing conditions had made them obsolete, and Veblen, like most of the relativists, wished to see the scientific method extended into the realm of moral philosophy. John Dewey, the chief spokesman of this school of thought, was similarly persuaded. His *The Quest for Certainty* (1929) asked: "how is science to be accepted and yet the realm of values to be conserved?" The answer was that values should *become* scientific. If men would only discard the notion that reality was something existing prior to and independent of knowledge, Dewey felt they could accept the relativistic, empirical way of making value judgments.

The intellectuals who lived in Greenwich Village have so frequently been termed iconoclastic and lost that it is surprising to find one of their leading spokesmen setting forth a Greenwich Village *creed*. Yet in *Exile's Return* Malcolm Cowley recalled that in the 1920s "Greenwich Village was not only a place, a mood, a way of life: . . . It was also a doctrine." Disregarding the charge that the Villagers had no ethics, Cowley itemized "new moral standards." There were eight central ideas. Three of them concerned individual freedom: "the idea of self-expression," "the idea of liberty," and "the idea of female equality." Cowley also listed "paganism," with its connotation of sexual release, and "the idea of living for the moment." His creed concluded by approving three methods of advancing freedom: educating children to be themselves, removing repressions with the aid of psychology, and living for a time in a foreign country.

Granted that these standards were not widely recognized as such in the American twenties, still in their own way Cowley and his Village colleagues were ethical beings. Indeed their emphasis on the dignity and sanctity of the individual was a very old and very central article in the American faith. The Village intellectuals were simply seeking new ways to give it expression.

There was a continuity of belief across the war years that weakens the lost generation hypothesis. A better image is that of a nervous generation holding tenaciously to one support until it could stretch and grasp another. Malcolm Cowley wrote wisely when he characterized his generation as belonging "to a period of transition from values already fixed to values that had to be created." The Humanists and other traditionalists, to be sure, did not even stretch; they just clung more tightly to the well-worn sanctions. For other intellectuals the basis of ethics shifted from the supernatural to the empirical, and from the permanent to the relative. But ethics themselves did not disappear. Indeed much of the substance of the new code that social science, relativism, and bohemian rebellion evolved bore a remarkable likeness to the old one.

Existentialism

While most intellectuals in the 1920s either reasserted or reconstructed familiar values, a few seemed gripped by thoroughgoing despair. Neither the old absolutes nor the new relativism sufficed for ordering existence. If anyone in the American twenties deserved the label lost, it was these apparent nihilists. But a second look, from the perspective of a period that knows existentialism, suggests that they were less adrift than has been supposed. Destruction of values, to be sure, proceeded apace. The bottom dropped out of Western belief. Yet the resulting doubt, disillusion, defeat, and despair became the bricks for constructing a new metaphysic. Its values were so different that they appeared to be no values at all. In protoexistential terms, however, failure and futility were prerequisites for investing life with meaning. John Dewey, who did not share the existential position, nevertheless understood the logic of the new faith. For the fringe of alienated intellectuals, he wrote in 1924, "skepticism became an ultimate exercise, something so certain that nothing could affect it. The mere act of doubting became a sacred rite; the performance of it afforded the requisite sense of the solid and unshakable."

Existentialism rests on the idea of the meaninglessness of human existence and the necessity of man's confronting that grim reality with unblinking frankness. By "meaningless," or as they sometimes say, "absurd," the existentialists attempt to articulate their conviction that life has no transcendent purpose, that traditional values are fraught with self-deception, and that finding happiness either rationally or romantically is futile. Death, they point out, is the inevitable, grinning end of all human endeavor. Man exists, in Søren Kierkegaard's nineteenth-century metaphor, as if he were alone in the ocean, miles from help, treading water seventy thousand fathoms deep. Nothing exists beyond the self. A person's inner, subjective existence is the starting point for perception. Man, in other words, partakes of no ideals, no realities, no essences of any kind external to the self. As the French philosopher Jean-Paul Sartre put it in 1945, "existence comes before essence . . . we must begin from the subjective."

The concept of alienation is crucial to existentialists like Sartre. They understand man as standing alone, alienated from any social or intellectual order. Thus he is totally free, completely self-dependent. In order to act existentially it is necessary to be lost.

According to the existentialists, the human predicament is that of having to keep sane in a hollow world, to resist suicide in the face of the purposelessness of life. The existential solution is twofold. First, each individual assumes total responsibility for his own life by the act of choosing between alternatives. He literally creates his own personal good and evil; he decides, in Sartre's phrase, between "being and nothingness." Each choice is consequently of ultimate importance. Total freedom and the necessity of choice, of making decisions, gives life meaning. Second, the existentialists accept the value of unbending struggle in the face of inevitable failure. The classic statement of this creed comes from another French thinker, Albert Camus. In *The Myth of Sisyphus* (1955) Camus has likened the human condition to that of a man repeatedly rolling a stone to a mountaintop only to have it fall down of its own weight. The effort is completely futile and hopeless. But because the roller of the rock realizes this and scorns his frustration, he achieves a certain victory, some dignity, and even a measure of happiness. The struggle alone and the courage it evokes are enough to give life meaning and value.

While Sartre and Camus formally stated the premises of modern existentialism in the 1940s and 1950s, certain American thinkers presaged the philosophy in the 1920s. Without adopting the name, they nonetheless began the search for existential meaning by cultivating an attitude of extreme disillusion. This alienated condition was essential to developing the complete individual responsibility that "existence comes before essence" demands. Being lost, and realizing it, was also necessary for creating a Sisyphean sense of value.

In this regard it is important to know that the phrase "lost generation" was not the invention of an historian or text-book writer. The intellectuals in question called themselves a lost generation. They found the concept useful and even appealing. They *wanted* to believe that they were lost, and they wanted others to believe it. It was fashionable and philosophically useful to affect a disillusioned posture, because being lost helped them make existential situations of their own lives. The alienated stance was a deliberate artistic construct, an attempt not to deny all values but to create a setting in which radically new, existential values could be formulated.

The way in which the actual phrase "lost generation" came into being is instructive. While the several accounts vary in details, there is a general consensus that the phrase originated with Gertrude Stein, the Radcliffe girl turned Parisian, and the unofficial dean of expatriated American artists and writers in Europe. There is also general agreement that Stein used the phrase in conversation with Ernest Hemingway about 1921. Hemingway's own account in *A Moveable Feast* is the most complete: Gertrude Stein, he begins, found it necessary to take her Model T Ford to a Paris garage for ignition repairs. Apparently the young mechanic who worked on the car did not fix it satisfactorily or possibly he took too long; Stein, at any rate, protested to the owner of the garage, and he in turn called the mechanic to task. The owner then explained to Stein that all the young workers in his shop lacked skill because they had served in the war and missed the crucial early years of vocational training. At one point in the conversation, according to Hemingway, the garage keeper said of his mechanics, that they were "all a *génération perdue*." Some time later Stein applied the phrase to the 23-year-old Hemingway and his friends. Angry at their rowdy, drunken behavior, she saw the connection: "'That's what you are. That's what you all are,' Miss Stein said, 'All of you young people who served in the war. You are a lost generation.'" Hemingway evidently was surprised; the idea had not occurred to him before. "'Really?'" he asked. " 'You are,' Stein insisted. 'You have no respect for anything. You drink yourselves to death. . . .' " Hemingway attempted to protest that he was never drunk when he came to the Stein salon, but Stein, as usual, had the final word: " 'Don't argue with me, Hemingway. . . . It does no good at all. You're all a lost generation, exactly as the garage keeper said.' "

At first Hemingway shrugged off the idea. "The hell with her lost-generation talk and all the dirty, easy labels," he thought as he walked home; it's "a lot of rot." But gradually Hemingway changed his mind. It was his genius to see that the war experience and the lost generation concept had esthetic and ethical possibilities. Indeed when he published his first novel, *The Sun Also Rises*, in 1926, he selected the garage keeper's phrase as his lead quotation. And the themes of alienation and futility pervade the book. Jake Barnes, the protagonist, castrated by a war injury, is symbolic of impotence. Yet Jake and his companions, drifting from bar to bar, achieve dignity in their failure, if only the dignity of facing the inevitability of failure with courage and grace.

The initiates in Hemingway's stories and novels have this talent. They are existentialists in fact, if not in name. They know the nothingness, the "nada" as Hemingway calls it, that exists outside those clean, well-lighted islands of meaning man vainly tries to create. They are obsessed with violence and pain because in the face of death life is stripped to its essence. External sugar-coatings drop away. Man stands terribly alone but free to choose his fate. Thus the figures of the matador in the bullring and the soldier on the battlefield recur repeatedly in Hemingway's writing. In existential terms such persons are at peace; their decisions give their life a personal meaning. In traditional terms Hemingway's heroes would not be considered heroic at all. But Hemingway was creating new rules for a new game. He posited the nonhero hero—one who stood out from the crowd not by attaining glory but by confronting failure.

Clutching around his shoulders the self-conceived mantle of the lost generation, and rather enjoying it, Hemingway prepared to use the war experience and the resulting despair to fashion a new philosophy of life. Existential protagonists fill his pages. One thinks of Brett Ashley in *The Sun Also Rises* who, in the face of the breakdown of all value and meaning, simply decides not to be a bitch. Or of Frederick Henry in *A Farewell to Arms* (1929) who, on learning of the death of both his lover and her new-born baby, neither cries nor prays nor commits suicide but walks slowly and stoically back to his hotel in the rain. Human existence, Hemingway suggests near the end of the book, is comparable to that of ants surrounded by a campfire. Some scatter and struggle frantically, others lie quietly, but none has a chance. Pain is a constant companion. Ultimately they wither in the heat and die. There is no purpose, no plan, no meaning in the annihilation. No one cares. Ethics, in the traditional sense, simply do not exist. The individual must make his own ethics by deciding how he will face the human condition.

And there are the minor Hemingway characters like Ole Andreson in "The Killers." Andreson had been a prize fighter who some time before double-crossed a mob of Chicago gangsters. In the story two thugs come to the small town where Andreson lives and announce their intention to settle the score. A boy, Hemingway's semi-autobiographical Nick Adams, overhears and slips away to warn the intended victim. When he arrives at Andreson's rooming house, he finds the huge boxer fully dressed lying on his bed. Excitedly Nick tells him of the killers and offers to get the police. But Andreson "looked at the wall. . . . 'There isn't anything I can do about it,'" he says. "'After a while I'll make up my mind to go out.'" Nick goes out with the big Swede still lying on the bed facing the wall. This is the existential way. Andreson acknowledges the certainty of death. He realizes the futility of trying to find conventional security and happiness by running away from the killers. His comfort and his dignity come from reserving the right to decide when he will leave the room and go out to face the guns.

Floyd Dell knew what Hemingway meant. A chief spokesman of the Greenwich Village intelligentsia, Dell attempted to summarize their creed in 1926. "Life, we felt, consisted so largely of spilt milk that there is no use crying over it—we might just as well celebrate the magnificent inevitability of the spilling."

In *This Side of Paradise* (1920) F. Scott Fitzgerald has created the often quoted portrait of Amory Blaine and his college-age contemporaries: "here was a new generation . . . grown up to find all Gods dead, all wars fought, all faiths in man shaken." The statement has been widely understood as defining the empty universe of the lost generation. Fitzgerald, however, is, like Hemingway, determined to salvage from the void some meaning and value for Amory and, presumably, for himself. His solution is to cast Amory in an existential stance. Fitzgerald begins by demonstrating the artificiality of Amory's existence as a romantic. We learn of Amory's belief in his own superiority and, when he cannot live up to his assumptions, his dreams of triumph. When separated from his girl friend, Isabel, he spends his evenings showing his devotion to her image by writing her rapturous letters. But the dream world is fragile; when he is reunited with Isabel, Amory sees that she is much less than he had conceived her to be.

In another relationship, with Rosalind, Amory assumes a realistic position and deprecates sentiment and romance. In response to her desire for them, Amory replies, "I never find anything else in the world and I loathe it." Yet as a realist he finds only emptiness. Even when he meets another girl who shares his ideas, he realizes that "their naked souls [were] poor things ever." Amory has thus rejected two forms of existence that are externally oriented, nonsubjective. The first, romanticism, perceives essence as an ideal or dream (however individual) which determines a person's existence. The second, realism, sees the barrenness of external reality but looks no further. In both cases the essence of a conception of objective reality determines the state of Amory's inner existence.

In the meantime Amory has become alienated from the values allegedly at stake in World War I. He is swept clean, ready to experiment with a new philosophy.

Operating in an ethical vacuum, Amory is called upon to make a sacrifice. Alec, a college friend, has brought a girl up to his hotel room. Amory, occupying the room next door, awakens to find his friend panic-stricken as policemen approach the room. There is no chance for escape. Knowing that he can, if he desires, make a sacrifice for his friend, Amory asks himself why he would want to. In the shadowed room he sees a brooding aura which he identifies as the devil, a force that has prevented him from taking certain actions in the past. Amory also sees, by the window, a vague figure he later realizes is the man who had given him a sense of religious values some years before. The two images persist as Amory confronts the choice at hand. Suddenly in a surge of joy he sees the images fade. The choice is now entirely his own, and he instructs Alec to act as if he were drunk. Amory accepts responsibility for being with the girl.

In the seconds between the policemen's knock and his decision Amory has reached a point of alienation from his former values. He has chosen for himself, and in existential terms he had found himself. Fitzgerald specifically points out that Amory realizes the sacrifice is impersonal; it cannot be attributed to any romantic dreams of heroism. Nor is it a realistic response to the situation, for, as a realist, Amory would have let Alec absorb the blame. Still Amory has made an ethical choice, and in so doing he has created an existential value. He has fashioned an essence from his existence alone.

Amory goes on from the hotel room episode to reject every creed extant in the 1920s. Failure, in the traditional sense, dogs his footsteps. He recognizes that his generation has "grown up to find all Gods dead." But Fitzgerald hastens to point out that Amory conceives of himself personally as blessed with a "new start." He can avoid moral suicide and cosmic despair. He can choose his own life knowing he is free from the hysteria around him. The last line of the novel seems to affirm beyond question Amory's existential stance. Beneath a "crystalline and radiant sky, Amory cries, 'I know myself but that is all.'" The final posture is that of the existentialist nonhero hero. Objectively, Amory is miserable, but he is free to possess himself.

Fitzgerald seemed to have a knack for concluding his novels on existential notes. *The Great Gatsby* (1925) ends: "so we beat on, boats against the current, borne back ceaselessly into the past." Here, too, there is the existential idea of futility and the idea of struggle; the inevitability of failure and the necessity of striving for success. It is unfortunate, in sum, that the Fitzgerald reputation is largely that of spokesman for a lost generation of nihilists and dissolutes. His writing on such themes, for instance the short stories of the early twenties that added "flapper" and "jazz age" to the American vocabulary, were never more than pot boilers written to keep the wolf from the Fitzgeralds' door. The other F. Scott Fitzgerald, the Fitzgerald of the novels, was a man engaged in a sensitive and serious search for morality and meaning. In a 1931 essay he remarked that the twenties were "an age of excess and an age of art." The excesses of intellectuals like Fitzgerald and Hemingway have been continually glamorized; their art should receive similar emphasis.

The force moving Hemingway and Fitzgerald toward existentialism was personal involvement in a world that seemed to them devoid of traditional kinds of meaning. Other American harbingers of existentialism in the 1920s took a more scholarly and longer-range view of the plight of modern man. In the broadest sense their problem was that of having seen scientific certainty itself collapse. The shock was severe. Man was left intellectually naked. The optimism of the Enlightenment and of nineteenth-century naturalism evaporated. Confidence in the ability of science to solve all problems and clarify values withered away. Such changes in physics could not fail to have an impact on metaphysics.

The traditional assumption of naturalism, the basis of its optimism, was the idea that regularities or laws existed in nature. These, in turn, made possible systematic understanding, prediction, and progress. Scientific truth, it was taken for granted, would replace the dogma and superstition of the past. Newton and Darwin had discovered ultimate, universal explanations. Increased knowledge led to greater happiness. There was order and purpose in the world. Indeed science had an absolutist character not unlike that of a religion. Nature might not be kind to man but at least it was comprehensible in its indifference.

Beginning in the late nineteenth century these assumptions received a series of jolts. De Vries and others questioned determinism in regard to biology. Rutherford destroyed simple concepts of atoms and matter. Planck showed the shortcomings of supposedly established mathematical truths. Millikan, Compton, and Einstein attacked the ultimate citadel of Newtonian physics. The chief shock, to be sure, came from Albert Einstein's special and general theories of relativity, set forth in 1905 and 1915 respectively. Einstein made so bold as to challenge existing concepts of time, space, matter, and energy. His essential point was that all motion was relative. With the exception of the velocity of light, which was constant, there was no such thing as absolute motion. Yet everything in the universe moved constantly, weight and size determining how fast. A yard was not a yard at 100,000 miles per second. It followed that there were no absolute standards or fixed points of reference. Einstein even contended that time was relative.

Under the impact of such thinking, Newtonian physics collapsed. The nature of gravity, on which Newton had grounded his system, changed radically. Einstein's ideas about atomic theory were likewise unsettling. If matter was composed of myriad moving, changing atoms, its permanent possession of certain properties was open to question. Also questionable, of course, was the validity of natural laws based on those properties. The overall effect of Einstein's work was to invest even the best-established scientific knowledge with an aura of uncertainty.

Most Americans, even most intellectuals, paid scant attention to this revolution in science. But its significance did not escape a few sensitive American minds. In 1927, for example, Percy W. Bridgeman, a Harvard physicist and philosopher, published *The Logic of Modern Physics*. Bridgeman recognized at the outset that Einstein's theories had come as a great shock to a scientific community basking in the assumed certainty of classical concepts. He went on to show that the work of Einstein and others made it imperative to abandon the entire notion of the existence of fixed properties of matter. Regularity of behavior was also untenable. Consequently, it was impossible to embrace all nature in "any formula, either simple or complicated." Einstein, according to Bridgeman, made it essential for scientists to recognize "the essential unpredictability of experiment beyond our present range." Natural laws, in other words, had only existed because man's knowledge was so limited. When it expanded, the certainties vanished. Writing in *Harper's* in 1929, Bridgeman summarized his conclusion: "The physicist finds himself in a world from which the bottom has dropped clean out; as he penetrates deeper and deeper it eludes him and fades away by the highly unsportsmanlike device of just becoming meaningless.... The world is not a world of reason, understandable by the intellect of man, but as we penetrate ever deeper the very law of cause and effect, which we had thought to be a formula to which we could force God himself to subscribe, ceases to have any meaning. The world is not intrinsically reasonable or understandable."

Alfred North Whitehead, the English logician who joined the Harvard faculty in 1924, was similarly persuaded that scientific abstractions applied only to themselves, not to real objects in nature. To assume otherwise, he declared in *Science and the Modern World* (1925), was to be guilty of "the fallacy of misplaced concreteness." Heretical as such ideas were in terms of the traditional scientific faith, they were the only conclusions possible to draw in the aftermath of the Einsteinian revolution. Naturalism and scientism had become self-defeating.

The American intellectual most articulate in his awareness of this situation was a young drama critic from Tennessee named Joseph Wood Krutch. In 1929 his book *The Modern Temper: A Study and a Confession* drew the full implications of the breakdown of science for American thought. The book's analysis was clearly existential, as

Krutch himself recognized in the 1950s when existentialism was known as such. His general thesis is simply stated: "the universe revealed by science . . . is one in which the human spirit cannot find a comfortable home." This realization, Krutch contended, was the basic reason for the mood of despair among intellectuals of the twenties. In his opening chapter Krutch compared nascent civilizations to children or to primitive savages. Each was characterized by unquestioning acceptance of life and unlimited, unthinking optimism. But as the child or the civilization grew older, experience and knowledge made life miserable. Both parties invented myths in an attempt to recapture the lost bliss. The child turned to winged horses and fire-breathing dragons; civilizations to love, god, morality, and free will. Increasing knowledge, however, did not support these myths. Metaphysics, with its concepts of progress and purpose, represented the world as man would *like* it to be; science revealed the world as it really was. And the two were irreconcilable. The rift between human ideals and the realities of existence was complete, and the human spirit was alienated from the natural universe. Morality, love, the social virtues could no longer be taken seriously. Science nowhere supported a sense of human dignity. "There is no reason to suppose," Krutch declared, "that [a man's] life has any more meaning than the life of the humblest insect that crawls from one annihilation to another." The verdict of science must be accepted: man is insignificant and nature indifferent.

"The Disillusion with the Laboratory" and "The Phantom of Certitude," Krutch's third and seventh chapters, extended his point that advances in scientific understanding ruthlessly undermined all belief in meaning and value. We could no longer even trust our senses. Vision showed us a table, for instance, which was solid and motionless. Yet atomic physics revealed that table to be a compound of dancing atoms, and relativity theory destroyed the certainty of its weight and size. There was, according to Krutch, no relation between man's inner world of perception and the outer world of science. Any conception of pattern, purpose, and goal was reduced, in Krutch's view, to a vain hope. As Henry Adams put it in his autobiography, published posthumously in 1918 and widely applauded by intellectuals of the 1920s, "Chaos was the law of nature; order was the dream of man." And Krutch, like Adams, saw fit to contrast this realization of twentieth-century man with the faith and security of his medieval predecessor. The villain, of course, was increased knowledge which had made any kind of metaphysics an absurdity.

Modern man, then, was reduced to an animal. Several thousand years of effort directed at giving meaning to life and rules for conduct were down the drain. But even from the depths of his dispair (which was, it must be emphasized, extreme among intellectuals of his time) Krutch came back to belief. The route was existential. First Krutch frankly confronted the human predicament. He submitted to alienation and purposelessness as inevitables. "Wisdom," as he has written in *The Modern Temper,* "must consist, not in searching for a means of escape which does not exist, but in making such peace with [futility] as we may." From this recognition of his wretchedness, Krutch moved toward existentialism. He chose to live alienated from the natural order despite the practical consequences, which might well be extinction. He deliberately chose the dream while knowing full well its hollowness. He would take full responsibility for his existence, and in so doing he achieved a kind of victory. "We may at least," he writes, "permit ourselves a certain *defiant* satisfaction when we realize that we have made our choice and are resolved to abide by the consequences." Krutch's Sisyphean rock was trying to be human as opposed to bestial. He knew he would fail, but, like Sisyphus, he did not despair of finding *some* meaning in life. The final sentences of the book distill the existential creed: "ours is a lost cause and there is no place for us in the natural universe, but we are not, for all that, sorry to be human. We should rather die as men than live as animals."

The handful of disillusioned intellectuals—really only a small fraction of the intellectual community—who constituted the self-proclaimed lost generation were not lost in the sense that they had no values. Neither were they resigned or dissipated. The old order and even the new science had crumbled around them, but still they searched, nervously, for meaning and value. Taking futility and despair for granted, the alienated few moved on toward the definition of a new kind of hero: a person who could face the inevitability of human failure with grace and courage. Certainly this posture was unglorious in traditional terms. Understandably those who adhered to older conceptions of value and valor found the nonhero hero incomprehensible. But the proponents of the new existential creed found in it an ideology with which life could, at least, be lived—and even lived with a certain dignity.

Chapter 4

The Mood of the People

Heroes

Heroes abounded in the American 1920s. Their names, especially in sports, have been ticked off so frequently they have become clichés. Less often have commentators paused to probe for explanations. Why were the twenties ripe for heroism? And why did the heroics follow a predictable pattern? Such questions lead to an understanding of the mood of the people, because heroism concerns the public as well as the individual. It depends on achievement but even more on recognition. In the final analysis the hopes and fears of everyday Americans create national heroes.

The nervousness of the post-World War I generation provided fertile soil for the growth of a particular kind of heroism. Many Americans felt uneasy as they experienced the transforming effects of population growth, urbanization, and economic change. On the one hand, these developments were welcome as steps in the direction of progress. Yet they also raised vague fears about the passing of frontier conditions, the loss of national vigor, and the eclipse of the individual in a mass society. Frederick Jackson Turner and Theodore Roosevelt, among others, had pointed to the liabilities of the transformation at the turn of the century. World War I underscored the misgivings and doubts. By the 1920s the sense of change had penetrated to the roots of popular thought. Scarcely an American was unaware that the frontier had vanished and that pioneering, in the traditional sense, was a thing of the past. Physical changes in the nation were undeniable. They occurred faster, however, than intellectual adjustment. Although Americans, in general, lived in a densely populated, urban-industrial civilization, a large part of their values remained rooted in the frontier, farm, and village. Exposure of this discrepancy only served to increase the tightness with which insecure people clung to the old certainties. Old-style pioneering was impossible, but Americans proved ingenious in finding equivalents. The upshot in the twenties was the cult of the hero—the man who provided living testimony of the power of courage, strength, and honor and of the efficacy of the self-reliant, rugged individual who seemed on the verge of becoming as irrelevant as the covered wagon.

Sports and the star athlete were the immediate beneficiaries of this frame of mind. The American sports fan regarded the playing field as a surrogate frontier; the athletic hero was the twentieth-century equivalent of the pathfinder or pioneer. In athletic competition, as on the frontier, people believed, men confronted tangible obstacles and overcame them with talent and determination. The action in each case was clean and direct; the goals, whether clearing forests or clearing the bases, easily perceived and immensely satisfying. Victory was the result of superior ability. The sports arena like the frontier was pregnant with opportunity for the individual. The start was equal and the best man won. Merit was rewarded. True or not, such a credo was almost instinctive with Americans. They packed the stadiums of the 1920s in a salute to time-honored virtues. With so much else about America changing rapidly, it was comforting to find in sports a ritualistic celebration of the major components of the national faith.

Writing in the *North American Review* for October 1929, A. A. Brill, a leading American psychologist of the Freudian school, took a closer look at the meaning of athletics. Why, he wondered, do men play and why do they select the particular kinds of play they do? Brill was also interested in the reasons spectators came to games. His main point was that sports were not idle diversions but intensely serious endeavors rooted in the values and traditions of a civilization. "The ancestry of sport," Brill declared, "is written very plainly in the fact that the first games among all nations were simple imitations of the typical acts of warriors and huntsmen." The primary motivation of play, according to Brill, was the "mastery impulse"—an inherent aggressiveness in man stemming from the Darwinian struggle for existence. Modern man had largely transcended direct physical struggle, but the need for it persisted in the human psyche. Sports were contrived as substitutes for actual fighting, mock struggles that satisfied the urge to conquer. Brill did not suggest a relationship between American sports and the American frontier, but his argument suggested one. So did the fact that the rise of mass spectator sports and the decline of the frontier were simultaneous in the United States.

By the 1920s the nation went sports crazy. It seemed to many that a golden age of sport had arrived in America. Football received a large portion of the limelight. As they had in the declining days of Rome, fans thronged the stadiums to witness contact, violence, bloodshed, man pitted against man, strength against strength. The vicarious element was invariably present. For a brief, glorious moment the nobody in the bleachers *was* the halfback crashing into the end zone with the winning touchdown. For a moment he shared the thrill of individual success and fought off the specter of being swallowed up in mass society.

Big-time professional football began on September 17, 1920, when the American Football Association was organized with the great Indian athlete Jim Thorpe as its first president. When the Green Bay Packers joined the Association in 1921, the saga of pro football was solidly launched. Attendance rose dramatically. On November 21, 1925, the presence on the playing field of the fabled Harold "Red" Grange helped draw 36,000 spectators to a game. A week later 68,000 jammed the Polo Grounds in New York to watch Grange in action. The names of the pro teams were suggestive. As on the frontier of old, it was cowboys versus Indians, or giants versus bears —with the names of cities prefixed.

The twenties was also the time of the emergence of college football on an unprecedented scale. Heroes appeared in good supply: Red Grange at Illinois, Knute Rockne's "Four Horsemen" at Notre Dame in 1924, Harold "Brick" Muller who began a dynasty at California that extended through fifty consecutive victories in the seasons 1919 through 1925. Hundreds of thousands attended the Saturday games, an estimated twenty million during the season. Millions more followed the action over their radios and made a Sunday morning ritual of devouring the newspaper accounts of the games of the previous day. To accommodate the crowds colleges and universities built huge new stadiums. Yale's and California's seated eighty thousand; Illinois, Ohio State, and Michigan were not far behind. The number of Americans who attended games doubled between 1921 and 1930. A *Harper's* writer caught the spirit of college football in 1928: "it is at present a religion, sometimes it seems to be almost our national religion." So, once, had been westward expansion.

Despite its popularity, football tended to obscure the heroic individual. It was, after all, a team sport. Even Red Grange received an occasional block on his long runs. But in sports pitting man against man or against the clock the heroism latent in competition achieved its purest expression. Americans in the 1920s had a glittering array of well-publicized individuals from which to choose their idol. In golf Robert T. "Bobby" Jones, Walter Hagen, and Gene Sarazen were the dominant figures. Tennis had "Big" Bill Tilden and "Little" Bill Johnson whose epic duels on the center court at Forest Hills filled the stands. The competition was even more direct in boxing with its "knock out," the symbol of complete conquest. During the twenties promoters like Tex Rickard built boxing into a big business. Jack Dempsey and Gene Tunney proved so attractive to the sporting public that a ticket sale of a million dollars for a single fight became a reality. By the end of the decade the figure was two million. Fifty bouts in the twenties had gates of more than $100,000. More than 100,000 fans came to Soldiers' Field in Chicago on September 22, 1927, to see the second Dempsey-Tunney fight with its controversial "long count" that helped Tunney retain the championship and earn $990,000 for thirty minutes of work. In a nation not oblivious to the approach of middle age, it was comforting to count the heavyweight champion of the world among the citizenry. Here was evidence, many reasoned, that the nation remained strong, young, and fit to survive in a Darwinian universe. Record-breaking served the same purpose, and in Johnny Weismuller, premier swimmer, and Paavo Nurmi, Finnish-born track star, the United States had athletes who set world marks almost every time they competed. Gertrude Ederle chose a longer course when she swam the English Channel in 1926, but she too set a record and was treated to one of New York's legendary ticker-tape parades.

And there was the Babe. No sports hero of the twenties and few of any decade had the reputation of George Herman Ruth. Baseball was generally acknowledged to be the national game, and Ruth played with a superb supporting cast of New York Yankees, but when he faced a pitcher Babe Ruth stood as an individual. His home runs (particularly the 59 in 1921 and the 60 in 1927) gave him a heroic stature comparable to that of legendary demigods like Odysseus, Beowulf, or Daniel Boone. Ruth's unsavory background and boorish personal habits were nicely overlooked by talented sportswriters anxious to give the twenties the kind of hero it craved. The payoff was public adulation of the Babe and of baseball.

The twenties also saw the public exposure of corruption in baseball and confronted Americans with the necessity of reviewing their entire hero complex. On September 28, 1920, three members of the Chicago White Sox appeared before a grand jury to confess that they and five other players had agreed to throw the 1919 World Series to Cincinnati for a financial consideration. Gradually the unhappy story of the "Black Sox" unfolded. Big-time gamblers had persuaded selected players to make sure that a bet on the underdog Cincinnati team would pay off. Some of the greatest names in the game were involved, preeminently that of "Shoeless" Joe Jackson. An illiterate farm boy from South Carolina, Jackson's natural batting eye helped him compile a .356 average in ten seasons as a major leaguer. In the process he became one of the most idolized players in baseball. It was Jackson's exit from the grand jury chamber on September 28 that allegedly precipitated the agonized plea from a group of boys: "Say it ain't so, Joe!" According to the newspapers, Jackson, shuffling, head down, replied, "Yes, boys, I'm afraid it is."

Reaction to the Black Sox testified to the importance baseball had for many Americans. One school of thought condemned the "fix" in the strongest terms and agitated for the restoration of integrity to the game. It was a serious matter. The Philadelphia *Bulletin* compared the eight players with "the soldier or sailor who would sell out his country and its flag in time of war." Suggesting the link between sports and the national character, the *New York Times* declared that bribing a ballplayer was an offense "which strikes at the very heart of this nation." If baseball fell from grace, what could be honest in America? The question haunted journalists and cartoonists. *Outlook* for October 13, 1920, carried a drawing of a crumpled statue of a ballplayer whose torn side revealed a stuffing of dollar bills. The statue bore the inscription "The National Game."

A small boy wept in the foreground; the caption to the cartoon read "His Idol."

Baseball officials and club owners were similarly dismayed at the revelation of corruption and determined to clean up the game. Charles A. Comiskey, owner of the Chicago White Sox, led the way with a public statement that no man involved in the fix would ever wear the uniform of his club again. Other owners followed suit until all organized baseball, even the minor leagues, was closed to the Black Sox. On November 12, 1920, Kenesaw Mountain Landis, a former federal judge, was appointed commissioner of baseball with full control over the game and a charge to safeguard its integrity.

The everyday fans' response to the fix differed sharply from that of the sportswriters and owners. Many Americans seemed determined to deny the entire affair; more precisely, they didn't *want* to believe anything could be wrong with something as close to the national ideal as baseball. Like the boys of the "say it ain't so" episode, they begged for evidence that the old standards and values still applied. Especially in 1920 in the United States sports heroes were needed as evidence of the virtues of competition, fair play, and the self-reliant individual. Consequently, when confronted with the scandal, the average American simply closed his eyes and pretended nothing was wrong. The heroes remained heroes. When the Black Sox formed an exhibition team, it received enthusiastic support. Petitions were circulated in the major league cities to reinstate the players in organized baseball. But the most remarkable demonstration of the public's feeling came at the conclusion of the Black Sox trial on August 2, 1921. After deliberating two hours and forty-seven minutes, the jury returned a verdict of *not* guilty. According to the *New York Times* reporter at the scene, the packed courtroom rose as one man at the good news, cheering wildly. Hats sailed and papers were thrown about in the delirium. Men shouted "hooray for the clean sox." The bailiffs pounded for order until, as the *Times* reported, they "finally noticed Judge Friend's smiles, and then joined in the whistling and cheering." Finally the jury picked up the acquitted ballplayers and carried them out of the courtroom on their shoulders!

Baseball officials and journalists regarded the acquittal of the Black Sox as a technical verdict secured by the lenient interpretation of the Illinois statute involved. The fans in the courtroom, however, and, presumably, many elsewhere were on the side of the players regardless, and viewed the verdict as a vindication. They were not prepared to believe that baseball or its heroes could become tarnished. The game was too important to the national ego. Following baseball gave Americans an opportunity to pay tribute to what many believed was the best part of their heritage. The game was a sacred rite undertaken not merely to determine the winner of league championships but to celebrate the values of a civilization. As one newspaper account of the scandal put it, to learn that "Shoeless" Joe Jackson had sold out the world series was like discovering that "Daniel Boone had been bought by the Indians to lose his fights in Kentucky."

In the gallery of popular heroes in the United States the only rival of the frontiersman and his athletic surrogate was the self-made man. In the 1920s the archtype was Herbert Hoover, a hero-President hewn out of the traditional rags-to-riches mold. Left an orphan in 1884 at the age of ten, Hoover launched an international career in mining that made him rich. During World War I he became famous, heading the American Relief Commission abroad and the Food Administration at home. A genius in matters of large-scale efficiency, Hoover neatly executed apparent miracles. After the decline of Woodrow Wilson in the wake of the Versailles Treaty, Hoover was easily the foremost American beneficiary of war-caused popularity. In 1922, while Secretary of Commerce under Warren G. Harding, he set forth his creed in a slender book entitled *American Individualism*. Apparently oblivious of the doubts that beset intellectuals at the time, Hoover professed his "abiding faith in the intelligence, the initiative, the character, the courage, and the divine touch in the individual." But he also believed that individuals differed greatly in energy, ability, and ambition. Some men inevitably rose to the top of the heap, and for Hoover this was entirely right and proper. It was necessary, moreover, if society were to progress. Hoover's philosophy was the old American one of rugged individualism and free enterprise that the Social Darwinists had decorated with scientific tinsel after the Civil War. Intellectually, Hoover was a bedfellow with Benjamin Franklin and William Graham Sumner.

Hoover's social, political, and economic ideas followed from these assumptions. He staunchly defended the unregulated profit system. Society and government owed the people only three things: "liberty, justice, and equality of opportunity." Competition took care of the rest, carrying the deserving to their just rewards and the failures to deserved defeat. Any interference, such as philanthropy to the poor or favoritism to the rich, only dulled *"the emery wheel of competition."* To be sure, Hoover paid lip service to restricting the strong in the interest of the society, but the main thrust of his thought awarded the victors their spoils. Critics were disarmed with three words—"equality of opportunity." The state should interfere to preserve it; otherwise, hands off! An exponent of the gospel of efficiency in economic affairs, Hoover believed that the road to the good life lay in the direction of more and better production. His mind equated material success with progress.

In the concluding chapter of *American Individualism*, Hoover drew the connection between his philosophy and the frontier. "The American pioneer," he declared, "is the epic expression of . . . individualism and the pioneer spirit is the response to the challenge of opportunity, to the challenge of nature, to the challenge of life, to the call of the frontier." Undismayed by the ending of the geographical frontier in the United States, Hoover declared that "there will always be a frontier to conquer or to hold to as long as men think, plan, and dare. . . . The days of the pioneer are not over."

When Hoover was elected President in 1928, these ideals were accorded the nation's highest accolade. They dominated popular thought as they had for three centuries of American history. In fact, all the men who occupied the Presidency from 1917 to 1930 were distinctly old-fashioned in their beliefs and in their public image. The traits are so familiar as to require listing only: Wilson the moralist and idealist; Harding the exemplar of small-town, "just folks" normalcy; Coolidge the frugal, farm-oriented Puritan; and Hoover the self-made man. If there was any correlation between a people's taste and its Presidents, then the record of this period underscored nostalgia.

Rivalling Hoover in the public mind of the early 1920s as an exponent of self-help and individualism was Edward Bok, the Dutch boy who made good and wrote about it in *The Americanization of Edward Bok* (1920). The book described Bok's immigration from Holland in 1870 at the age of six and his rise from a fifty-cents-a-week window cleaner to editor of the magazine with the largest circulation in the nation, the *Ladies Home Journal*. Bok's autobiography reads as a paean to the American ideal of success. Through luck, pluck, and clean living, he became a confidant and friend of Presidents. Thrift and determination made him rich. Bok played the rags to riches theme to the hilt. "Here was a little Dutch boy," he wrote in his preface, "unceremoniously set down in America . . . yet, it must be confessed, he achieved." His book, Bok promised, would describe "how such a boy, with every disadvantage to overcome, was able . . . to 'make good.' "

In the final chapters of his autobiography, Bok stepped back to comment on the liabilities and advantages of America. He did not slight the former, yet in "What I Owe to America" Bok brushed all debits aside in order to celebrate America's gift of "limitless opportunity: here a man can go as far as his abilities will carry him." For anyone "endowed with honest endeavor, ceaseless industry, and the ability to carry through, . . . the way is wide open to the will to succeed."

The public reception of *The Americanization of Edward Bok* suggests how much Americans in the 1920s wanted to confirm old beliefs. Bok was a hero in the Benjamin Franklin-Horatio Alger mold. His success story demonstrated that passing time and changing conditions had not altered hallowed ideals. His pages suggested no troubling doubts, and, after receiving the Pulitzer Prize for biography in 1921, Bok's book became a best-seller. An inexpensive eighth edition issued in July 1921 enabled it to attain third place on the 1922 lists. But the primary reason for Bok's popularity as hero-author was his ability to tell a nervous generation what it wanted to hear.

It has long puzzled students of the Great Crash of 1929 why even the most informed observers in education and government as well as business did not recognize and heed the prior economic danger signals that in retrospect seem so apparent. Part of the explanation possibly lies in the depth of the general commitment to the ideals of rugged individualism and free enterprise that Hoover and Bok articulated and symbolized. This commitment, in turn, lay in the nervousness of the American people. So much about the twenties was new and disturbing that Americans tended to cling tightly to familiar economic forms. They just could not bear to admit that the old business premises based on individualism and free enterprise might be fraught with peril. With Herbert Hoover leading the way, they chose to go down with the economic ship rather than question and alter its suicidal course.

Respect for the old-time hero was evident in other aspects of postwar thought. The vogue of the Boy Scouts is an example. Although the movement began in 1910, the twenties was the time of its flowering. There were 245,000 Scouts at the beginning of 1917, 942,500 at the end of 1929. In addition, 275,000 adults volunteered their services as leaders. No youth club and few adult organizations matched this record. The Boy Scout Handbook, a manual of ideals and instruction, sold millions of copies. Scouting, apparently, tapped fertile soil in its embodiment of the old-time idea of good citizenship and expertise in the outdoors. The Scout, standing straight in his shorts or knickers and doing the daily good deed that his oath required, was the epitome of the traditional American model of heroic young manhood.

In the late 1920s the Boy Scout *Handbook* featured an unusual drawing. In the foreground was a clean-cut Scout, eyes fixed on adventure. Behind him, signifying the heritage from which he sprang, were the figures of Daniel Boone, Abraham Lincoln, and Theodore Roosevelt, men who were staples in the annals of American heroism. But there was also a new face, that of Charles A. Lindbergh of Minnesota. At the age of just twenty-five Lindbergh rose to the status of an American demigod by virtue of a single feat. On May 20, 1927, he took off in a tiny single-engine airplane from New York City and thirty-three hours later landed in Paris. The nonstop, solo run across the Atlantic catapulted the average American into a paroxysm of pride and joy. Overnight Lindbergh became the greatest hero of the decade. There was but little exaggeration in the contention of one journalist that Lindbergh received "the greatest ovation in history." Certainly his return from Paris to the United States generated a reception extraordinary even for an age that specialized in ballyhoo. The *New York Times* devoted more space to Lindbergh's return than it had to the Armistice ending World War I. A virtual national religion took shape around Lindbergh's person. A 1928 poll of schoolboys in a typical American town on the question of whom they most wanted to be like produced the following results: Gene Tunney, 13 votes; John Pershing, 14; Alfred E. Smith, 16; Thomas A. Edison, 27; Henry Ford, 66; Calvin Coolidge, 110; Charles A. Lindbergh, 363. If the amount of national adulation is meaningful, adults everywhere would likely have responded in similar proportions.

The explanation of Lindbergh's popularity lies less in his feat (pilots had flown across the Atlantic before) and more in the mood of the people at the time it occurred. The typical American in 1927 was nervous. The values by which he ordered his life seemed in jeopardy of being swept away by the force of growth and change and complexity. Lindbergh came as a restorative tonic. He reasserted the image of the confident, quietly courageous, and self-reliant individual. He proved to a generation anxious for proof that Americans were still capable of pioneering. Even in an age of machines the frontier was not dead—a new one had been found in the air.

The reaction to Lindbergh's flight in the national press stressed these ideas. "Lindbergh served as a metaphor," wrote one commentator in *Century*. "We felt that in him we, too, had conquered something and regained lost ground." A writer in *Outlook* made the point more explicitly: "Charles Lindbergh is the heir of all that we like to think is best in America. He is the stuff out of which have been made the pioneers that opened up the wilderness first on the Atlantic coast, and then in our great West." A newspaper cartoon showed a covered wagon leaving for California in 1849 and next to it Lindbergh's plane taking off for Paris in 1927. Colonel Theodore Roosevelt, the son of the President, remarked that Lindbergh "personifies the daring of youth. Daniel Boone, David Crockett, and men of that type played a lone hand and made America. Lindbergh is their lineal descendant." Calvin Coolidge, who personally welcomed Lindbergh home, simply said that he was "a boy representing the best traditions of this country."

For one journalist the most significant part of the Lindbergh phenomenon was not the flight but the character of the man: "his courage, his modesty, his self-control, his sanity, his thoughtfulness of others, his fine sense of proportion, his loyalty, his unswerving adherence to the course that seemed right." His unassuming manner fit the traditional hero's mold. Many observers of the postflight celebration noted how the hero refused to capitalize financially on his popularity. It was telling evidence as an essayist put it, that the American people "are *not* rotten at the core, but morally sound and sweet and good!" The generalization from the individual to society was easily acceptable because Americans in 1927 desperately wanted to keep the old creed alive. Lindbergh's flight was popularly interpreted as a flight of faith—in the American experience and in the American people.

Looking back over the 1920s F. Scott Fitzgerald remembered in

1931 that "in the spring of 1927, something bright and alien flashed across the sky. A young Minnesotan who seemed to have nothing to do with his generation did a heroic thing, and for a moment people set down their glasses in country clubs and speakeasies and thought of their old best dreams." Also in 1931 Frederick Lewis Allen recalled that Lindbergh had been "a modern Galahad for a generation which had foresworn Galahads." Both Fitzgerald and Allen were right in their assessment of the public reaction to Lindbergh's flight, but wrong about the dreams he engendered being foreign to the 1920s. Fitzgerald notwithstanding, Lindbergh had a great deal to do with his generation. Allen to the contrary, the Lindbergh craze was not a case of Americans returning to ideals they had forsaken; they had never left them.

Books

Popular books as well as heroes revealed the American mind in the 1920s, and the great majority of the best-sellers of the decade were decidedly old-fashioned. Frontier and rural patterns of thought and action dominated the popular novels. Their plots and protagonists operated according to time-honored standards of competition, loyalty, and rugged individualism. Complications were few and usually resolved, in the final pages, with an application of traditional morality. The total effect was a comforting reaffirmation of the old American faith. Such novels, to be sure, made slight contribution to serious American literature. But they were read—by millions! And they both influenced and reflected the mood of Americans who had never even heard of Fitzgerald and Hemingway. Indeed in comparison to best-selling authors, the Fitzgeralds and Hemingways were highly esoteric.

Exact figures are elusive, but it would be difficult to dispute Gene (Geneva) Stratton-Porter's claim to preeminence among popular novelists in the first three decades of the twentieth century. Her vogue began with *Freckles* in 1904 and continued right through the war, into the twenties, and beyond. In 1932 a *Publisher's Weekly* survey of the best-selling novels of the century revealed Porter in the top four positions with *Freckles, The Girl of the Limberlost* (1909), *The Harvester* (1911), and *Laddie* (1913). Each had sold well over a million copies. With other titles Porter made the "top ten" list in 1918, 1919, 1921, and 1925. Most of her sales were in fifty-cent reprint editions, suggesting that her public consisted of relatively unsophisticated readers.

Gene Stratton-Porter found a publishing bonanza by articulating the values to which a large part of the American reading public subscribed. Chief among them was a belief in the virtue of close association with nature. As a girl Porter ran in the swamps, woods, and fields around Wabash, Indiana, and the characters in her novels do likewise. The experience was represented as inspirational in the highest sense. Nature was not only a source of beauty and contentment but a repository of moral and religious truth. The outdoors provided a constant backdrop in Porter's stories. Indeed the margins of her books were sometimes adorned with pen and ink drawings of birds, animals, and flowers. *The Harvesters* was dedicated to Henry David Thoreau.

Second only to nature in Porter's scale of values was cheerfulness. Her stories expound the benefits of optimism, confidence, courage, and keeping a stiff upper lip. Typically the plots involve the protagonist, frequently a child, in a series of adversities. But looking for the silver lining and heeding the teachings of nature eventually resolve all problems. *Freckles*, for instance, describes a boy who believes himself an orphan, wanders in the Limberlost swamp, and is ultimately found and claimed by his wealthy father. Eleanora of *A Girl of the Limberlost* defies poverty by selling the moths she collected in the swamp. In *Michael O'Halloran* Porter copied the Horatio Alger formula, taking a little newsboy up the success ladder on the wings of determination and pluck.

Porter's novels appealed to the kind of American whose eyes glazed and even dampened when they thought of the good old days when life was simple and generally lived in close proximity to nature. In Porter one basked momentarily in an uncomplicated world where virtue triumphed and right prevailed. Much of Porter's public seemed to consist of people displaced or crushed by modern American civilization. Letters of appreciation poured in to her from sanitariums, rest homes, reform schools, and jails. But in a larger sense the uncertainties and nervousness of the age in general provided a milieu in which her kind of writing could flourish.

William Lyon Phelps once wrote of Gene Stratton-Porter, "she is a public institution, like Yellowstone Park, and I should not think she would care any more than a mountain for adverse criticism." In fact, Porter did care. She habitually replied to her unfavorable reviewers in lengthy letters. In one she responded to a critic who had labelled her writing "molasses fiction." This was really a compliment, rejoined Porter: "molasses is more necessary to the happiness of human and beast than vinegar.... I am a molasses person myself. ... So I shall keep straight on writing of the love and joy of life... and when I have used the last drop of my molasses, I shall stop writing." She closed the letter with a hint of conceit: "God gave me a taste for sweets and the sales of the books I write prove that a few other people are similar to me in this."

Harold Bell Wright rivaled Gene Stratton-Porter as a dispenser of wholesomeness, optimism, and the arcadian myth. His *The Winning of Barbara Worth* (1911) had a half million copies in print within a month of its initial publication and maintained sufficient popularity to rank fifth, behind Porter's four books, in the 1932 best-selling novels of the century poll. After *Barbara Worth* Wright produced a novel every other year for two decades. Americans seemed as eager to buy and read his books after the war as before. His first twelve books enjoyed an average sale of nearly 750,000 each.

A sometime minister, Wright sermonized constantly in his novels. Until the final typing no character in any had a name except that of his main trait—Hypocrisy, Greed, Ambition, and so on. Wright's message was the familiar one: clean living, hard work, and contact with God's great open spaces could save a man from the physical and moral deterioration city life engendered. *When a Man's a Man* of 1916, for example, features a millionaire who goes west to escape the effete, artificial, decadent East. Its setting on an Arizona cattle ranch reflected Wright's own enthusiasm for the Southwest that led him to make his home there. Wright also loved Missouri's Ozark Mountains, and the region figured in a number of his stories. *The Re-Creation of Brian Kent*, third on the best-seller list for 1920, employs an Ozark setting to tell the story of a human wreck who is redeemed by the beauty of nature, the challenge of work, and a woman's love. An elderly schoolmarm, identified only as Auntie Sue, supervises the transformation and extracts the moral.

The stereotyped plots and characters, the wooden dialogue, and the commonplace preaching in Wright's books elicited a barrage of unfavorable criticism. According to one reviewer in 1924, Wright was guilty of perpetuating "the shibboleths and superstitions of our fathers, making old creeds and antique fables sacred in the eyes of all." And so he did. Yet his stories sold millions of copies. A large number of American readers found his message comfortable and meaningful. "Harold," one critic punned, "is always Wright." But for the popular mind of the teens and twenties ethical certainty was highly valued, and traditional mores seemed the most certain. The intellectuals might scoff, but Wright, like Porter, found the gold-mine of popular favor.

The western novel, which Owen Wister introduced into American writing in 1902 with *The Virginian,* increased in popularity as the nation moved increasingly further from frontier conditions. The foremost practitioner of the art in the decade after World War I was a one-time dentist from Zanesville, Ohio, named Zane Grey. Blend-ing minor literary talent with a keen sense of the public taste, Grey produced over fifty westerns and provided the basis for dozens of motion pictures, many of which were produced in the early 1920s before the advent of sound tracks. The total sale of all his writings approaches twenty million. From 1917 to 1924 Grey was never *off* the national list of the top ten best-sellers. Twice, 1918 and 1920, he ranked first. He may well have been the most widely read author in the American twenties.

The Zane Grey magic was a blend of violence, heroism, and the frontier. His stories lacked sophistication, but they juxtaposed good and evil in unmistakable terms. Titanic struggles might be waged, but the issues were always clearly defined and the outcome, as Grey fans came to learn, never really in doubt. A simple code of conduct suffused Grey's books. It emphasized courage, self-reliance, fair play, and persistence—the traditional frontier virtues. Those who violated the code always paid the price.

As a mythmaker for the multitudes in the 1920s, Zane Grey be-came as legendary as his protagonists. Many people believed he spoke for the best parts of the national heritage. John Wanamaker, the department store mogul, addressed him directly: "never lay down your pen, Zane Grey. . . . You are distinctively and genuinely American. You have borrowed none of the decadence of foreign writers. . . . The good you are doing is incalculable." Even the critics treated Grey more tolerantly than they did Porter and Wright. "We turn to him," one commentator wrote, "not for insight into human nature and human problems nor for refinements of art, but simply for crude epic stories, as we might to an old Norse skald, maker of the sagas of the folk."

The concept of escape from the present, so important in the appeal of many of the best-selling popular novels in the twenties, reached a climax in the writing of Edgar Rice Burroughs. A failure for years in business and pulp magazine writing, Burroughs turned to a new theme in 1914 and struck pure gold. *Tarzan of the Apes* has probably sold more copies to date (over five million) than any other American book. Over thirty other stories of the English orphan reared in the African jungle by apes followed. As early as 1920 the Tarzan cult was nationwide. Burroughs was syndicated in newspapers; his motion pictures reached millions of people. With his superhuman prowess and his mate, Jane, Tarzan entered public thought and speech to an astonishing degree. For people vaguely repressed by civilization, Tarzan was a potent symbol of freedom, power, and individuality. A new wild man on a new frontier, Tarzan helped sustain traditional American values.

American readers seemed to have an unsatiable appetite for nature novels in the first three decades of the twentieth century. In addition to Porter, Wright, Grey, and Burroughs, a host of others rode the theme to publishing successes that were minor only in comparison. The names of Rex Beach, Peter B. Kyne, Emerson Hough, and James Oliver Curwood were quite familiar to readers and moviegoers of the postwar decade even if they are not to most literary historians. Curwood, for instance, published between 1908 and 1926 twenty-six novels that dramatized the theme of courage in the wilderness. The motion pictures made from his books, such as *Back to God's Country* (1919), were intended, so an advertisement ran, for those who "love God's great out-of-doors, the land of frozen forests and everlasting snows where the gaunt wolf stalks its prey, where men loom large and life is big." In 1923 Hough's *The Covered Wagon* became the basis for the most famous western movie of the decade. Stewart Edward White rivalled both Curwood and Hough with books such as *The Blazed Trail, The Silent Places,* and *The Rules of the Game.* And that was it precisely—the game had rules that were at once easily perceived and rooted in the national character. If changing conditions were eroding the old certainties, that was only more reason to grasp them more tightly.

In popular fiction Americans of the 1920s were still inhabitants of the nineteenth century. The sexy novels of flaming youth and the risqué movies satisfied only part of the taste of the twenties. The other, and larger, part thrilled to old-time heroics such as those provided by the man Douglas Durkin sketched in *The Lobstick Trail* of 1922: "his blood was clean, his body knit of fibre woven in God's out-of-doors, his mind fashioned under a clear sky in a land of wide horizons."

Crusades

An examination of some of the more prominent social and political crusades of the 1920s reveals other aspects of the conservatism of the popular mind. When Americans became sufficiently agitated to organize in these years it was usually because they believed traditional standards and values were threatened. Morality (the nineteenth-century variety) and Americanism were the most common objectives of citizen action. The defense of both indicated a need for absolutes, and the hysterical tone of the defense suggested that in some quarters the need was desperate. Bigoted and preposterous as the crusaders seem in retrospect, and corrupt as some of the leaders were, many of the people involved were in deadly earnest. In their minds the dangers were real and their patriotism or moralism genuine. Apathetic? Hedonistic? Liberated? On the contrary, the crusaders' way of thinking suggests a degree of sincerity and a need for security totally out of keeping with the reputation of the 1920s.

The first evidence that anxiety produced more rather than less reliance on old values was the crusade for 100 per cent Americanism during World War I and the subsequent Red Scare. In this case the nation was the reed to which nervous people clung. George Creel and his wartime Committee on Public Information made nationalism a religion (see page 50). An official government agency, the CPI dealt in both loyalty and hatred. The Four Minute Men made speeches that deified America and vilified Germany. Making unprecedented use of propaganda, Creel and his colleagues reached the lowest levels of popular thought. Action followed. In July 1918 over a hundred thousand persons were seized in Chicago alone; twenty thousand suspected of un-Americanism were detained. Americans rediscovered the security of having and hounding an enemy.

With the end of World War I, American paranoia shifted its focus of attention from the Germans to the "Reds." The Bolshevik Revolution in Russia of November 1917 and the subsequent revolutionary uprising in other parts of the world seemed to many Americans to presage the overthrow of their own order. A series of highly-publicized strikes and bombings in early 1919 further whetted fears. By autumn millions thought revolution in the United States was imminent. The setting was right for a crusade against communism. With the support of public opinion behind him, A. Mitchell Palmer, Wilson's Attorney General, had thousands of known and suspected radicals arrested. Over 550 were deported according to Palmer's formula of "ship or shoot." Nationalism, uncooled from the recent war, ran to extremes. An Indiana jury, for example, required but two minutes to *acquit* a man who had killed another for yelling "to hell with the United States!" In Chicago Mayor William Hale Thompson found that flamboyant patriotism could nicely cover inefficiency and corruption. Throughout the country dispensers of 100 per cent Americanism like the American Legion and the Daughters of the American Revolution found new sources of support.

The distorted nativism of nervous minds continued into the 1920s under the white gowns and masks of the second edition of the Ku Klux Klan. Launched in 1915 by a never-say-die Southerner, the KKK rose to nationwide power in the early twenties. It offered ritual, hierarchy, secrecy, uniforms—all the paraphernalia so dear to nervous men—but the heart of the Klan was hatred. In this, at least, it did not discriminate. Jews, Catholics, Negroes, immigrants, urbanites, "wets," and liberals were attacked with equal venom. The typical Klansman was of the lower social and economic classes, lived in a village or rural region in the South or Middle West, and felt threatened by growth and change. He was the antithesis of the roaring twenties image, and he was not uncommon. Between 1920 and 1924 the KKK grew from five thousand members to an estimated five million. It became a major political force in at least a dozen states. While clever advertising techniques accounted for some of this success, the uneasy mood of the people was the basic explanation.

It is as easy as it is common to dismiss the Ku Klux Klan as an infantile and psychotic aberration devoid of ideals and values. And indisputably some Klan leaders, like the notorious David C. Stephenson of Indiana, were the worst sort of opportunists. Yet the Klan expressed the attitudes of a sizable and otherwise inarticulate portion of American society. In the minds of millions of grass roots members and sympathizers, the KKK was a bastion of cherished beliefs, a sincere response of well-meaning people to disturbing conditions and slipping standards. It was a response, moreover, that reflected the hold of traditional ethics on the popular mind of the twenties. The Klan regarded itself as the custodian of the national morality—America's front line of defense against evil, degeneracy, and, as it frequently turned out, modernism.

Hiram Wesley Evans, one-time dentist and Imperial Wizard of the KKK, made this clear in an article in *North American Review* for March, 1926. Writing under the title "The Klan's Fight for Americanism," he defined the intellectual achievement of his organization. It had gained recognition for "the idea of preserving and developing America first and chiefly for the benefit of the children of the pioneers ... and ... along the lines of the purpose and spirit of those pioneers." Evans rightly explained the Klan as "an idea, a faith, a purpose, an organized crusade." The main portion of Evans' article marshalled Madison Grant, Lothrop Stoddard, and other racist intellectuals (see pages 69–72) in support of the idea that racism was only "sane and progressive conservatism" of "old stock Americans" applied to "the work of preserving and developing our American traditions and customs." The rise of the Klan, Evans felt, was simply a response to the "moral breakdown" of the past two decades. "One by one all our traditional moral standards went by the boards."

The mind of the Klansman was absolutist. He craved clear-cut standards and sharp distinctions between right and wrong. Klan spokesmen left no doubt on this point. As one stated, "every criminal, every gambler, every thug, ... every girl runner, ... every wife beater, ... every moonshiner, every crooked politician, ... is fighting the Klan. Think it over. Which side are you on?" Such a Manichaean perspective favored quick, violent solutions to problems like those provided by the lash or lynching noose. Nervous about the present and fearful about the future, the Klansman yearned for an allegedly simpler and purer past.

The major institutional expression of nervous nativism was the passage of a series of federal laws restricting immigration. The first, in 1917, imposed a literacy requirement on those seeking to emigrate to the United States. It failed, however, to check the tide. In 1920–1921 1,235,000 foreigners entered the country. Congress responded to public concern with a 1921 act limiting the number of immigrants from any given country to 3 per cent of those in America in 1910.

Although a sharp reduction in immigration followed, calls for greater restriction persisted. In 1924 Coolidge signed the Immigration Act further curtailing the flow of "undesirable" newcomers with quotas based on national origin. "America," said Coolidge on the occasion of the act's passage, "must be kept American." If a large proportion of his contemporaries had not felt the same, it is difficult to imagine that such legislation could have been enacted. As it was, immigration restriction testified to the anxieties of many Americans.

Another sign that old ideals and ethics still retained their vigor in the 1920s was prohibition. The amount of publicity given then and now to violations of the Volstead Act has frequently obscured the plain fact that it *was* national law throughout the decade. Indeed the jazz age was the only decade in American history to institute the policy. A large number of Americans and their representatives, we must conclude, believed in its desirability and deplored its ineffectiveness. For them it really was a "noble experiment." This is not, of course, to deny that other millions regarded prohibition as a joke or that a drink could be bought almost anywhere in the country during the twenties with relative ease. It is simply to recognize that there was dissention in American thought on the drinking question and that at least part of the national mind was not liberated from older restraints and ethics.

While enforcement of the Volstead Act after its inception on January 17, 1920, proved virtually impossible, the "drys" did not weaken in their convictions. Their crusade ran strong up to 1929. In their minds prohibition was an outgrowth of the Progressive faith in implementing the American dream through legislation. For the drys drinking was not only the root of most social evil but a symbol of cities, sexual freedom, and the eroding ethics of modern life in general. Again and again the spokesmen of the Anti-Saloon League and the Women's Christian Temperance Union suggested that the stakes in the battle with the wets were not just alcohol but the republic itself. For them prohibition was a way of expressing a preference for a stricter moral order and a cleaner, simpler nation such as existed in their memories of the past. The election of 1928 phrased the issue clearly in the dry mind, and their man won. Only after the Crash of the following year did sufficient national opinion swing against prohibition to cause its downfall.

Americans of the twenties also participated in less organized movements. One had moral decency as its object. Like the drys, the moralists have not received attention commensurate with their numbers or importance. Flaming youth, after all, makes better copy than the behavior and attitude of more repressed Americans. Moreover, in reporting the morality of the twenties, dream has been confused with reality. The millions who gasped at films like *Her Purchase Price*, relished sex scandals like the Hall-Mills case, and bought Bernarr Macfadden's *True Story Magazine* had nothing even remotely comparable in their own lives—hence the fascination. Neither, it seems safe to say, did every flapper who talked freely of sexual relations engage in them with equal casualness. The amount of smoke in such matters always exceeded the amount of fire. Virgins just did not vanish in the 1920s, even if attitudes toward them shifted slightly in some quarters. The revolution in morals, in sum, has been exaggerated out of all proportion to both its prevalence and its depth.

A strong current of old-fashioned morality ran right through the roaring twenties. It appeared in the vogue of Emily Post's guidebooks to etiquette, in the campaigns to enforce minimum coverage standards for bathing suits, and in the attempt during the so-called jazz age to repress this music as too charged with erotic connotations. Traditional morality was also evident in the solemn crusades to ban books and censor movies. There were results, too, as in 1923 when the motion picture industry responded to broad public pressure by appointing William H. Hays, Postmaster General in the Harding administration, to the position of censor. Hays promptly developed a code consisting of "two feet on the floor" rules for bedroom scenes and similar restrictions. Reluctant as it was to check itself, Hollywood recognized better than some historians that the level of frankness the public would tolerate was still quite low.

Every commentator on the American twenties has noted the rise of the hem line throughout the decade and linked it to the emergence of the American woman. Certain elements in American society, however, fought undress inch by inch. Rural fundamentalists joined urban gentry in urging moderation in dress and deportment. The clergy of fifteen denominations endorsed a "moral gown" with elbow-length sleeves and a hem precisely seven and one-half inches above the floor. In countless families parents sparred with children on the question of sex relations. For every girl at a petting party, however innocuous, there were two worriers—a ratio that those responsible for the reputation of the 1920s have failed to appreciate.

Faith

The 1920s have seldom been considered an age of faith, and yet on the popular level religion proved a potent influence on the thought of the decade. Sincere religiosity in the decade has been persistently misinterpreted. Bruce Barton, for example, has been wrongly represented to several generations of students as a businessman-writer whose works illustrated the secularization and dilution of Christianity in the postwar years. Countless lecturers as well as many books have quoted Barton's statement that "Jesus picked up twelve men from the bottom ranks of society and forged them into an organization that conquered the world" as evidence that the twenties were so commercially minded that even religion was construed in business terms. Barton's assertions that Jesus was "the most popular dinner guest in Jerusalem" and that the parables were "the most powerful advertisements of all time" have been put to similar purpose. Religion, it is suggested, was valued only as good business. "Each hour spent in wholesome, Christian self-improvement," a university president is quoted, "is worth $10,000." The conclusion usually drawn is that Americans in the 1920s repudiated traditional religious guidelines in mad pursuit of gain.

A second look, however, leaves quite a different impression. Bruce Barton's three best-selling books, *The Man Nobody Knows* (1924), *The Book Nobody Knows* (1926), and *What Can a Man Believe?* (1927) were actually celebrations of Christianity and efforts to make it more, not less, relevant to modern America. Barton was a partner in the high-powered advertising firm of Batten, Barton, Durstine and Osborn, but he was also the son of a preacher, a graduate of years of Sunday school, and an adult of deep religious convictions. Believing religion indispensable to a full life, Barton long lamented that no professional clergyman saw fit to modernize ancient doctrine to fit current circumstances. Finally he undertook the task himself. His first book contended that the greatness of Jesus lay in his strength, his charisma, his drive. *The Man Nobody Knows* "redesigned" the image of Christ from a meek and lowly man into a sun-tanned, hard-muscled giant. The purpose was not to mock but to praise. When Barton likened Jesus to a successful businessman, he was only creating a metaphor that he believed would be meaningful to his contemporaries. There was no intent to sanctify business. Jesus, according to Barton, "led the most successful life on this planet" but remained poor. Christ's achievement was in love, not sales. Barton further maintained that the much-publicized Protestant ethic referred to the process, not the product, of business. Money was always secondary. Barton, in sum, provides better evidence for the rise of interest in religion in the 1920s than for its decline. And, presumably, the Americans who made *The Man Nobody Knows* the fourth best-selling work of nonfiction in 1925 and the first in 1926 were likewise attracted to, rather than repelled by, faith.

In the mid-twenties, when most travelers used trains and religious controversies were making headlines, Henry Mencken quipped: "heave an egg out of a Pullman and you will hit a Fundamentalist almost everywhere in the United States." The remark has been used to document the alleged disgust and cynicism of intellectuals, and it does testify to Mencken's personal animosity for farmers, but it also suggests the prevalence of religious fundamentalists in the American twenties.

As much of the familiar intellectual terrain around them seemed to quake, a sizable number of Americans nervously clung to old-time religion. The Bible served as a comforting, unquestioned absolute. Here was stability in an age of seeming change, security at a time of nervousness. The Rock of Ages grew in significance as investigations into the ages of rocks raised disconcerting questions. Better to give blind allegiance to the old certainties than to admit frightening new possibilities. Fundamentalism was a doctrine which stood against any change in religious orthodoxy. It postulated the infallibility of Scripture, the love and mercy of Jesus Christ, the imminence of the second coming, and the reality of heavenly salvation. The faithful did not question these fundamentals. Miracles, of course, were a staple in the fundamentalists' religious diet, and the whole philosophy exuded a sense of hope, confidence, triumph, and joy. It was a simple faith answering a basic human need.

Chuckle and rail at these ideas as they might, sophisticated religious liberals were unable to shake the commitment of a large number of Americans in the 1920s. Even full-scale debate, such as the famous Scopes Trial of 1925, did not kill fundamentalism. Clarence Darrow, defending John Thomas Scopes against charges of teaching the evolutionary version of creation in Tennessee public schools, claimed that William Jennings Bryan, the leader of the prosecution, held "fool ideas that no intelligent Christian on earth believes." But there must have been substantial numbers of "unintelligent" Christians in the United States—the verdict in the trial, after all, was "Guilty," and laws prohibiting the teaching of evolution remained (and still do) in the statutes of several states. Bryan, moreover, was not crushed and broken by the experience in Tennessee as commonly supposed. At his death, five days after the Scopes Trial, he was happily and eagerly preparing his undelivered closing speech for national distribution. And as his funeral train made its way slowly across the upper South on its way to Washington, D.C., hundreds of thousands gathered along the tracks to pay tribute to Bryan's memory and ideals. Mencken's egg would have hit many a fundamentalist.

While Bryan was only a part-time defender of the faith, the postwar years saw several popular religious leaders rocket into national prominence. Among these revivalists with a fundamentalist message was a one-time professional baseball player whose real name was Billy Sunday. In 1914 he ranked eighth in a national opinion poll on the greatest man in the United States. His popularity continued into and through the war. Presidents paid him tribute. John D. Rockefeller referred to him in 1917 as "a rallying center around whom all people interested in good things may gather." As World War I increased popular anxieties, Sunday's appeal broadened. The largest of his more than three hundred organized revivals were concentrated in the period 1916–1921. Over a million people came to hear him flail at jazz, bootlegging, evolution, and the new morality. "America," he often said, "needs a tidal wave of Old-Time Religion." Crass as his methods were, Sunday met the needs of one segment of American society. His influence on the nation's religious life in the immediate postwar years was undeniable.

As Sunday's star began to fade in the mid-twenties, a new one rose. Aimee Semple McPherson was the first major female revivalist in American religious history. Born in 1890 and converted at seventeen by an itinerant evangelist whom she promptly married, Aimee entered evangelical work herself in 1916. For several years she drifted on the revival circuit from Maine to Florida and began to publish *The Bridal Call*, a small monthly newspaper. Fundamentalist in tone, it underscored the infallibility of the Bible, the blessings of conversion, faith healing, miracles, and the love of Christ. Her market was specific, if broad. "I bring spiritual consolation to the middle class," she declared, "leaving those above to themselves and those below to the Salvation Army." In 1918 Aimee staged a successful revival in Los Angeles. Sensing the hunger of that city's displaced Southerners and Midwesterners for her message of love and belonging, she chose it for the base of her operations. Her stadium-sized Angeles Temple opened in 1923 in a suburb of Los Angeles as the hub of a $350,000-a-year business. By this time Aimee was calling her doctrine the Four Square Gospel. The numerical reference was to the four cherubim in Ezekiel, representing the Savior, baptism, healing, and the Second Coming. It was, in Aimee's opinion, "a perfect gospel. A complete gospel for body, for soul, for spirit, and for eternity." There were also four pillars of her creed: God, home, school, and government. "Remove any one of these," she warned, "and [civilization] topples, crumbles."

The core of the Four Square Gospel was individual salvation. Through iron will and hard work any man could remake his life along godly lines. The reformed sinner was Exhibit A in Aimee's church as he had been in those of earlier American revivalists. While avoiding some of the excesses of the pietistic tradition, the Four Square Gospel still demanded an emotional confrontation of the individual with the Savior. Aimee played upon hope rather than fear. "Who cares about old Hell, friends?" she asked in a typical sermon. "Why we all know what Hell is. We've heard about it all our lives. A terrible place where nobody wants to go. I think the less we hear about Hell the better, don't you? Let's forget about Hell. Lift up your hearts. What *we* are interested in, yes, Lord, is *Heaven*, and how to get there!" This was old-time religion. Aimee did not mince words: "in religion, I am really a fundamentalist," she stated in 1928.

The key to Aimee Semple McPherson's success as an evangelist was the way she combined an old message with modern tastes and techniques. She blended styles. What the Four Square Gospel offered, essentially, was a religious vaudeville, a spectacle worthy of Hollywood. Over five thousand people jammed the Angeles Temple every evening for Aimee's service. Thousands more followed the proceedings over radio station K F[our] S[quare] G[ospel], owned by the church. Seldom were the expectant throngs disappointed. Orchestras and choruses thundered out a variety of secular as well as sacred music. Sermons were often animated, as "The Green Light Is On," which featured Aimee roaring down the aisle on a motorcycle, or "The Merry Go Round Broke Down" with Aimee as the mechanic who saved the day. In "Throw Out the Life Line!" a dozen nightgowned maidens, clinging to the Rock of Ages amidst crashing thunder and flashing lightning, were pulled across the stage to safety by sailors of the Lord. On another occasion Aimee dramatized the triumph of Good over Evil with a huge electric scoreboard. Props like a throne bedecked with a thousand carnations were regular fare at the Temple.

Still the heart of every service, and indeed of the entire Four Square Gospel, was the woman herself. Possessed of unusual beauty and sensuality in addition to charisma, Aimee Semple McPherson exploited her physical gifts to the fullest. Typically she entered the Temple, after a carefully timed delay, through a small door high on the wall. A soft spotlight picked out her white robe, rich auburn (when it was not dyed blonde) hair, bouquet of flowers, and white leather Bible. Gracefully she swept down to the throne. It was a moving experience even for objective observers. One reporter, critical of the Four Square Gospel movement, had to confess "she is a beautiful woman, seen from the auditorium.... Let no man venture to deny it.... The writer has seen screen beauties in his day, and confesses to a slight clutch of the heart as he watched her superb entrance." Outside the church Aimee was equally striking. She once arrived in Los Angeles from London wearing an ermine coat with fox trim, a brown cloche, tan stockings, and black shoes. On another occasion in Egypt she donned exotic native garb for a photograph astride a camel.

The Americans who responded to the Four Square Gospel, and there were (and still are) many thousands, found Aimee Semple McPherson's weaving of the old and new attractive. She gave them the best of both worlds—a simple, hopeful, authoritarian faith and "whoopee" salted with just the right amount of sex. While the Four Square Gospel raised paeans to godliness and old-fashioned morality, Aimee herself careened through a series of spectacular marital and financial misadventures. She was married three times, widowed once, and divorced twice. A total of fifty-five suits were entered against her for a variety of damages. She warred with her mother and ultimately ousted her from the church. In 1926 Aimee made the front pages of newspapers across the country when her "disappearance" (she actually enjoyed a month at a secret retreat with a lover) was followed by her "resurrection" in Mexico and an implausible kidnapping story. But the Four Square Gospelers did not seem to mind. They thrived on news of Aimee's risqué personal life and at the same time joined her in deploring jazz age morality. Piety served as whitewash. Aimee put sex and spectacle in a safe container where people who did not quite dare to be modern could enjoy them. She dressed old ideas in new clothes. She was grandmother and flapper simultaneously. Characterizations of her as "the Barnum of religion" and "the Mary Pickford of revivalism" hit the mark precisely. She rose to popularity on the wings of public ambivalence.

Chapter 5

Henry Ford: Symbol of an Age

Few names were better known to Americans from 1917 to 1930 than that of Henry Ford. Whether one read his publications,[1] or followed his headline-making public life, or merely drove the car his company manufactured, Ford was inescapable in the twenties. Indeed it is possible to think of these years as the automobile age and Henry Ford as its czar. The flivver, along with the flask and the flapper, seemed to represent the 1920s in the minds of its people as well as its historians.

Cars symbolized change. They upset familiar patterns of living, working, recreating, even thinking. Much of the roar of the twenties came from the internal combustion engine. While providing portable bedrooms in which to enjoy the decade's alleged sexual freedom, cars also assisted gangsters and bootleggers in getting away. The image of two of them in every garage helped elect a President in 1928. The rise of widespread use of the automobile, in

---

[1] In all probability Henry Ford did not actually write the numerous books, pamphlets, and articles associated with his name and attributed to him in this chapter. He was not a literary man; his critics even alleged he could not read! But Ford could pay people to express his opinions for him, and there is no reason to think that the ideas these writers recorded were not those of their employer.

a word, contributed significantly to setting the twenties apart. And Henry Ford, calling machinery the "new Messiah" (as he did in 1929), seemed to herald the new era.

Beneath the surface, however, such generalizations ring hollow. Neither Ford nor the twenties merited the clichés with which each has been so frequently discussed. In the case of the man, both old and new mingled in his mind. On the one hand Ford was a builder and bulwark of the modern, mechanized nation; on the other he devoted a remarkable amount of effort and expense to sustaining old-fashioned America. In fact, the nostalgic, backward-looking Henry Ford repeatedly deplored the very conditions that Ford the revolutionary industrialist did so much to bring about. This ambivalence did not signify a lack of values so much as a superfluity. His faith was strong if bigoted and contradictory. His prescriptions for America were clear if simple-minded. He seemed to the masses to demonstate that there could be change without disruption, and in so doing he eased the twenties' tensions. "The average citizen," editorialized the *New Republic* in 1923, "sees Ford as a sort of enlarged crayon portrait of himself; the man able to fulfill his own suppressed desires, who has achieved enormous riches, fame and power without departing from the pioneer-and-homespun tradition." In this nervous clinging to old values even while undermining them Ford was indeed a "crayon portrait" of his age.

But was Ford typical of the twenties? Can he really be said to symbolize the age? He was, after all, in his middle fifties when the decade began. However, a great many Americans were also middle-aged in the 1920s, far more in fact than the twenty-year-old collegians who have hitherto characterized these years. And at one point even a group of college students ranked Ford as the third greatest figure of all time, behind Napoleon and Jesus Christ.

The Dearborn, Michigan, into which Henry Ford was born in 1863 was a small farming community only a generation removed from the frontier. Both sides of the Ford family had agrarian backgrounds, and the children grew up on the farm. Henry's formal education began and ended in the Scotch Settlement School which he attended for eight years. The staple of his academic diet was the McGuffey reader with its moral-coated language lessons. When Ford left school to become an apprentice mechanic in Detroit, he also left the farm. But the farm never left Henry. Agrarian ideas and values shaped his thought even as he became an industrial king.

The 1880s for Ford were a time of aimlessness, his only real interest being in tinkering with watches and other engines. In 1892 he joined the Edison Company in Detroit as an engineer. During his spare time he struggled with the problem of building a gasoline engine compact enough to power a moving vehicle. By 1896 Ford had his automobile. Soon he had it doing ninety miles per hour! It required seven years more, however, for him to secure the necessary financial and administrative backing to launch the Ford Motor Company. The rest was pure Horatio Alger.

The first Model T appeared in 1908, and it soon made good Ford's boast that he could build a car for the masses. Six thousand sold the first year. Six years later, after the introduction of assembly line production, the figure was 248,000. From May to December 1920 almost 700,000 Model Ts rolled out of the Ford plants. The total for 1921 was one million. In 1923 57 per cent of all cars manufactured in the United States were Fords. Three years later the Ford Motor Company produced its thirteen millionth car. From the perspective of efficient production the Ford organization was also something of a miracle. In 1913 it required twelve hours to make a car. The following year, after the introduction of the assembly line techniques, the figure dropped to ninety-three minutes. In 1920 Ford achieved his long-time dream of building one car for every minute of the working day. And still he was unsatisfied. On October 31, 1925, the Ford Motor Company manufactured 9,109 Model Ts, one every ten seconds. This was the high point, and competition was rising to challenge Ford's preeminence, but by the end of the twenties Henry Ford was a legend, a folk hero, and reputedly the richest man who ever lived. Transcending the role of automobile manufacturer, he had become an international symbol of the new industrialism. The Germans coined a word to describe the revolutionary mass production techniques: *Fordismus*. At home Ford's popularity reached the point where he could be seriously considered a presidential possibility for the election of 1924.

Fortunately for the historian of his thought, if not always for himself, Henry Ford had a propensity for forthrightly stating his opinions on a wide variety of subjects outside his field of competence. He also had the money to publish and otherwise implement his ideas. The resulting intellectual portrait was that of a mind steeped in traditional Americanism. For Ford agrarian simplicity, McGuffey morality, and Algerian determination were sacred objects.

Nationalism was writ large over all Ford did, and America was great because of its heritage of freedom, fairness, and hard, honest work. Ford's confidence in the beneficence of old-fashioned virtues verged on the fanatical. The "spirit of '76," equal opportunity democracy, rugged individualism, the home, and motherhood were Ford's touchstones of reality. He deified pioneer ethics and values. "More men are beaten than fail," he declared in 1928. "It is not wisdom they need, or money, or brilliance, or pull, but just plain gristle and bone." A decade earlier "Mr. Ford's Page" in the *Dearborn Independent* stated that "one of the great things about the American people is that they are pioneers." This idea led easily to American messianism. "No one can contemplate the nation to which we belong," the editorial continued, "without realizing the distinctive prophetic character of its obvious mission to the world. We are pioneers. We are the pathfinders. We are the road-builders. We are the guides, the vanguards of Humanity." Theodore Roosevelt and Woodrow Wilson had said as much, but Ford was writing *after* the war that allegedly ended the nation's innocence and mocked its mission.

Ford's intense commitment to the traditional American faith led him to suspect and ultimately to detest whatever was un-American. The same loyalties compelled him to search for explanations for the unpleasant aspects of the American 1920s that exonerated the old-time, "native" citizen. The immigrant, and particularly the Jew, were primary targets of Ford's fire. In editorial after editorial in the *Dearborn Independent* and in several books Ford argued that aliens who had no knowledge of "the principles which have made our civilization" were responsible for its "marked deterioration" in the 1920s. They were, moreover, determined to take over the country if not the world. Spurred by such fears, Ford became a subscriber to the tired legend of an international Jewish conspiracy. When he couldn't find sufficient evidence for such a plot, Ford dispatched a number of special detectives to probe the affairs of prominent Jews and collect documentation. The search resulted in the "discovery" of the so-called "Protocols of the Learned Elders of Zion," an alleged exposition of the scheme by which the Jews planned to overthrow Gentile domination. Although the "Protocols" was exposed as a forgery in 1921, Ford continued to use the spurious document to substantiate his anti-Semitism until late in the decade. Everything wrong with modern American civilization, from the corruption of music to the corruption of baseball, was attributed to Jewish influence. Unable to admit that America as a whole might be blamed for its problems, unwilling to question the beneficence of time-honored ways, Ford searched for a scapegoat. He found it in the newcomers who, he believed, had no conception of or appreciation for American ideals.

The tension in Henry Ford's thought between old and new, between a belief in progress and a tendency to nostalgia, is dramatically illustrated in his attitude toward farming and farmers. On the one hand he believed farm life to be a ceaseless round of inefficient drudgery. Indeed, he had abundant personal evidence, remarking at one point, "I have traveled ten thousand miles behind a plow. I hated the grueling grind of farm work." With the incentive of sparing others this painful experience, Ford addressed himself to the problem of industrializing agriculture. The farmer, in Ford's opinion, should become a technician and a businessman. Tractors (Ford's, of course) should replace horses. Mechanization would make it possible to produce in twenty-five working days what formerly required an entire year. Fences would come down and vast economies of scale take place. Ford's modern farmer would not even need to live on his farm but instead could commute from a city home. To give substance to these ideals Ford bought and operated with astonishing success a nine-thousand-acre farm near Dearborn.

Still Ford, the "Father of Modern Agriculture," as he has been dubbed, was only part of the man. He also retained a strong streak of old-fashioned, horse-and-buggy agrarianism. Farming, from this standpoint, was more than a challenge in production; it was a moral act. Constantly in the twenties, even while he was helping make it possible, Ford branded the modern city a "pestiferous growth." He delighted in contrasting the "unnatural," "twisted," and "cooped up" lives of city-dwellers with the "wholesome" life of "independence" and "sterling honesty" that the farm environment offered. In Ford's view the importance of cities in the nation's development had been greatly exaggerated. Early in the 1920s the *Dearborn Independent* editorialized: "when we all stand up and sing, 'My Country 'Tis of Thee,' we seldom think of the cities. Indeed, in that old national hymn there are no references to the city at all. It sings of rocks and rivers and hills—the great American Out-of-Doors. And that is really The Country. That is, the country is THE Country. The real United States lies outside the cities."

As such a manifesto suggests, a bias toward nature and rural conditions was an important element in Henry Ford's thought. "What children and adults need," he told one reporter, "is a chance to breathe God's fresh air and to stretch their legs and have a little garden in the soil." This ideal led Ford to choose small towns instead of cities as the sites of his factories. "Turning back to village industry," as Ford put it in 1926, would enable people to reestablish a sense of community—with nature and with men—that urbanization had destroyed. Ford believed that cities were doomed as Americans discovered the advantages of country life.

Ford's enthusiasm for nature did not stop with ruralism. From 1914 to 1924 he sought a more complete escape from civilization on a series of camping trips with Thomas A. Edison. John Burroughs, the naturalist, and Harvey Firestone, the tire king, also participated. Although the equipment these self-styled vagabonds took into the woods was far from primitive, they apparently shared a genuine love of the outdoors. In the words of Burroughs, they "cheerfully endure wet, cold, smoke, mosquitoes, black flies, and sleepless nights, just to touch naked reality once more." Ford had a special fondness for birds. With typical exuberance he had five hundred birdhouses built on his Michigan farm, including one with seventy-six apartments which he called, appropriately, a "bird hotel." There were also electric heaters and electric brooders for Ford's fortunate birds. The whole production mixed technology and nature in a way that symbolized Ford's ambivalence. When he could not camp or visit his aviary, Ford liked to read about the natural world. Indeed he preferred the works of Emerson, Thoreau, and Burroughs to the Bible. Ford so admired Burroughs' variety of natural history that even before becoming acquainted with him he sent him a new Ford car.

As for roads and automobiles, Ford saw them not as a threat to natural conditions but rather as a way for the average American to come into contact with nature. The machine and the garden were not incompatible. "I will build a motor car for the great multitude . . . ," Ford boasted, "so low in price that no man . . . will be unable to own one—and enjoy with his family the blessings of hours of pleasure in God's great open spaces." In *My Life and Work* of 1923 Ford again confronted the tension between nature and modern civilization. He declared that he did not agree with those who saw mechanization leading to a "cold, metallic sort of world in which great factories will drive away the trees, the flowers, the birds and the green fields." According to Ford, "unless we know more about machines and their use . . . we cannot have the time to enjoy the trees and the birds, and the flowers, and the green fields." Such reconciliations only partially covered Ford's nervousness about the mechanized, urbanized future. Contradictions persisted in his thinking. The same man who envisaged fenceless bonanza farms could say, "I love to walk across country and jump fences." The lover of trees could state in utmost seriousness, "better wood can be made than is grown."

Ford's attitude toward history has been subject to wide misunderstanding. The principal source of confusion is a statement Ford made in 1919 at the trial resulting from his libel suit against the *Chicago Tribune*. "History," he declared, "is more or less the bunk. It is tradition. We don't want tradition. We want to live in the present, and the only history that is worth a tinker's dam is the history we make today." On another occasion he admitted that he "wouldn't give a nickel for all the history in the world." Complementing this sentiment is Ford's reputation as a forward-looking inventor and revolutionary industrialist unsatisfied with the old processes. Here seems a man fully at home in the alleged new era of the 1920s. But in fact Ford idolized the past. His "history . . . is bunk" remark came in response to a question about ancient history and Napoleon Bonaparte and had reference to written history. For history itself—what actually happened in his nation's past and its tangible evidence—Ford had only praise.

The most obvious evidence of Ford's enthusiasm for history was his collector's instinct. He began with that bastion of his own youth, the McGuffey readers. Sending agents out to scour the countryside and putting aside considerations of cost, Ford owned by 1925 one of the few complete collections of the many McGuffey editions. Hoping to share his treasures with his contemporaries, Ford had five thousand copies of *Old Favorites from the McGuffey Readers* printed in 1926. The book contained such classic stories as "Try, Try Again" and "The Hare and the Tortoise." It dispensed an ideal of individualism and self-reliance at the same time that Ford's assembly lines were making men cogs in an impersonal machine.

From books Ford turned to things, and during the 1920s amassed a remarkable collection of American antiques. He bought so widely and so aggressively that he became a major factor in prices in the antique market. Everything was fair game. Lamps and dolls, bells and grandfather clocks made their way to Dearborn. Size was no problem. Ford gathered enough machines to show the evolution of the threshing operation from 1849 to the 1920s. Another exhibit traced the development of wagons in America. Eventually the entire heterogeneous collection went into the Edison Museum at Dearborn, a pretentious building designed to resemble, simultaneously, Independence Hall, Congress Hall, and the old City Hall of Philadelphia. Ford delighted in showing visitors around the five-acre layout. Asked on one occasion why he collected, Ford replied, "so that they will not be lost to America." Later, on the same tour, Ford played a few bars on an antique organ and observed, "that takes me back to my boyhood days. They were beautiful days."

This sentiment undoubtedly figured in Ford's 1920 decision to restore his boyhood home. Everything had to be exactly as he remembered it. Furniture, china, and rugs were rehabilitated or reconstructed. Ford even used archaeological techniques to recover artifacts around the family homestead. The ground was dug to a depth of six feet and the silverware, wheels, and other equipment used by his parents in the 1860s were recovered. In 1922 Ford purchased the Wayside Inn at Sudbury, Massachusetts, to preserve it from destruction. Celebrated by the poet Henry Wadsworth Longfellow, the old inn appealed to Ford as a symbol of pioneer days. He opened it for the public's edification in 1924. But a new highway ran too near. Roaring cars disturbed the horse-and-buggy atmosphere. So, turning against the age he helped create, Ford had the state highway rerouted around the shrine at a cost of $250,000. He also bought and restored the schoolhouse in Sudbury alleged to be the site where Mary and her little lamb gamboled. Naturally the shop of the "Village Blacksmith," also in Sudbury, had to be included in Ford's antique empire.

Beginning in 1926 with the construction of Greenfield Village near Dearborn, Ford embarked on a career of large-scale historical restoration. This time not a building but a whole community was the object of his attention. Greenfield, named after the Michigan hamlet in which Ford's mother grew up, was a monument to his agrarianism as well as his reverence for the past. "I am trying in a small way," Ford explained with unwarranted modesty, "to help America take a step ... toward the saner and sweeter idea of life that prevailed in pre-war days." Greenfield Village had gravel roads, gas street lamps, a grassy common, and an old-fashioned country store. The automobile mogul permitted only horse-drawn vehicles on the premises. The genius of assembly line mass production engaged a glass blower, blacksmith, and cobbler to practice their obsolete crafts in the traditional manner. Ford dispatched his agents to seek out, purchase, and transport to Greenfield the cottages of Walt Whitman, Noah Webster, and Patrick Henry. In time they even secured the crowning glory: the log cabin in which William Holmes McGuffey had been born and raised.

History, then, was not "bunk" to Henry Ford. The speed of change seemed to increase proportionately his desire to retain contact with the past. As Ford declared in 1928, a year before completing Greenfield Village, "improvements have been coming so quickly that the past is being lost to the rising generation." To counter this tendency Ford labored to put history into a form "where it may be seen and felt." But values and attitudes were also on display. Ford looked back with nostalgia to the pioneer ethic. With it, he believed, the nation had been sound, wholesome, happy, and secure. "The Old Ways," as the *Dearborn Independent* declared, "Were Good."

Ford's opinion of the new morality of the jazz age was, not surprisingly, low. He deplored the use of tobacco and even went so far as to publish for mass circulation a tract, entitled *The Case Against the Little White Slaver*, which excoriated cigarettes. When Ford had the power he went beyond exhortation. "No one smokes in the Ford industries," their leader proclaimed in 1929. As for alcohol, Ford was equally unyielding. Twice he threatened to make his international labor force teetotalers at the risk of their jobs. In his American plants Ford enforced a policy of abstinence. Any workman detected drinking publicly or even keeping liquor at home was subject to dismissal. The prohibition policy of the 1920s, in Ford's estimation, was a great triumph. "There are a million boys growing up in the United States," he exulted in 1929, "who have never seen a saloon and who will never know the handicap of liquor." When confronted with evidence of widespread violation of the Nineteenth Amendment, Ford had a ready explanation. A Jewish conspiracy was to blame for illicit booze. The mass of real Americans, Ford believed, were, like himself, dry by moral conviction as well as by law.

Sex was too delicate a matter to be addressed directly, but Ford conveyed his opinions through a discussion of music and dancing.

Few aspects of the American 1920s worried him more than the evils of jazz. The new music clashed squarely with his ruralism and Bible-belt morality. In 1921 Ford struck out in anger at "the waves upon waves of musical slush that invade decent parlors and set the young people of this generation imitating the drivel of morons." Organized Jewry, once again, was blamed for the musical degeneracy. "The mush, the slush, the sly suggestion, the abandoned sensuousness of sliding notes," declared the *Dearborn Independent,* "are of Jewish origin." The problem, obviously, was not only musical but sexual as well. The loosening of morals in the 1920s appalled Ford. He expressed his feeling in reference to jazz: "monkey talk, jungle squeals, grunts and squeaks and gasps suggestive of cave love are camouflaged by a few feverish notes." What Ford could only bring himself to call "the thing" appeared also in song titles such as *In Room 202* and *Sugar Baby.* Pointing to the Jewish origin of these tunes (Irving Berlin was a frequent target of attack), Ford called on his countrymen to crush the serpent in their midst.

The reform of dancing fitted nicely into Ford's campaign to elevate the nation's morals to old-time standards. His interest began with the collection of traditional folk dances. Not only the scores but the backwoods fiddlers themselves were invited to Dearborn to play *Old Zip Coon* and *Arkansas Traveler.* To Ford's delight, here was something both wholesome and historical. He also manifested concern over social dancing, publishing in 1926 a guidebook entitled *"Good Morning": After a Sleep of Twenty-five Years Old-Fashioned Dancing is Being Revived by Mr. and Mrs. Henry Ford.* The book also endeavored to revive old-fashioned morality. It began by condemning as promiscuous the newer dances such as the Charleston and the whole flapper syndrome. "A gentleman," the book explained, "should be able to guide his partner through a dance without embracing her as if he were her lover." Proper deportment, according to Ford, minimized physical contact. "[The gentleman's] right hand should be placed at his partner's waist, thumb and forefinger alone touching her—that is, the hand being in the position of holding a pencil." There were also rules regarding gloves, handkerchiefs, and the way to request a partner for a dance. Ford's dance manual, in short, was a monument to the old conceptions of morality, decorum, and order, and the dances he and his wife hosted at Dearborn were implementations. Precisely at nine Ford's guests convened in evening dress in a lavish ballroom for a paean to Victorianism.

Ambivalence is the key to the mind of Henry Ford. He was both old and new; he looked both forward and backward. Confidently progressive as he was in some respects, he remained nervous about new ways. The more conditions changed, the more the nostalgic Ford groped for the security of traditional values and institutions. He was not lost; on the contrary, he had too many gods, at least for consistency. Neither was he dissipated and roaring. And he hated jazz. But Ford was popular, indeed a national deity, in the twenties even if his senatorial and presidential bids fell short. As a plain, honest, old-fashioned billionaire, a technological genius who loved to camp out, he seemed to his contemporaries to resolve the moral dilemmas of the age. Like Charles A. Lindbergh, another god of the age, Ford testified to the nation's ability to move into the future without losing the values of the past.

A Note on the Sources

The length and nature of Chapter II and the frequent mention of titles in the text partially obviates the need for an extended bibliography. The few entries here will at least suggest my extensive debt to others.

A good vantage point for beginning advanced study of the thought of the period are the historiographical essays: Henry F. May, "Shifting Perspectives on the 1920's," *Mississippi Valley Historical Review*, 43 (Dec., 1956), 405–427; John D. Hicks, "Research Opportunities in the 1920's," *Historian*, 25 (Nov., 1962), 1–13; Hicks, *Normalcy and Reaction, 1921–1933*, Service Center for Teachers of History Publication, No. 32 (1960); Burl Noggle, "The Twenties: A New Historiographical Frontier," *Journal of American History*, 53 (Sept., 1966), 299–314; Don S. Kirschner, "Conflicts and Politics in the 1920's: Historiography and Prospects," *Mid-America*, 48 (Oct., 1966), 219–233; and Richard W. Lowitt, "The Prosperity Decade, 1917–1928," in William H. Cartwright and Richard L. Watson, Jr., eds., *Interpreting and Teaching American History* (1961), pp. 231–263.

From here one might turn to the rich secondary studies in American intellectual history (both high and low) written during or shortly after the period in question: Harold E. Stearns, ed., *Civilization in the United States: An Inquiry by Thirty Americans* (1922); Freda Kirchwey, ed., *Our Changing Morality: A Symposium* (1924); Robert S. and Helen M. Lynd, *Middletown: A Study in Contemporary American Culture* (1929); President's Research Committee on Social Trends, *Recent Social Trends in the United States*, 2 vols. (1933).

Comprehensive studies that proved indispensable for the present synthesis were: Frederick J. Hoffman, *The 20's: American Writing in the Postwar Decade*, rev. ed. (1962); Robert E. Spiller, et al., *Literary History of the United States*, 3 vols., rev. ed. (1963); Alfred Kazin, *On Native Ground: An Interpretation of Modern American Prose Literature* (1942); Morton G. White, *Social Thought in America: The Revolt against Formalism*, rev. ed. (1957); William E. Leuchtenberg, *The Perils of Prosperity, 1914–1932* (1958); Merle Curti, *The Growth of American Thought*, 3rd ed. (1964); Paul Carter, *The Twenties in America* (1968); Henry Steele Commager, *The American Mind; An Interpreta-*

tion of American Thought and Character since the 1880s (1950); Arthur
M. Schlesinger, Jr., *The Age of Roosevelt, I: The Crisis of the Old
Order, 1919–1933* (1957); Stow Persons, *American Minds* (1958);
David Van Tassel, ed., *American Thought in the Twentieth Century*
(1967); Herbert W. Schneider, *A History of American Philosophy*, 2nd
ed. (1963); Ralph Henry Gabriel, *The Course of American Democratic
Thought*, 2nd ed. (1956); Oscar Cargill, *Intellectual America: The
March of Ideas* (1941); Russel B. Nye, *This Almost Chosen People*
(1966); and Archibald MacLeish, "There Was Something About the
Twenties," *Saturday Review*, 49 (Dec. 31, 1966), 10–13.

Although Malcolm Cowley's *Exile's Return: A Narrative of Ideas*, rev.
ed. (1951) is in some senses an autobiography, it contains enough
valuable comment on the intellectual life of others in the 1920s to
warrent inclusion in this list of secondary sources.

John Braeman, Robert H. Bremner, and David Brody, eds., *Change
and Continuity in Twentieth-Century America: The 1920's* (1968) is a
collection of original essays many of which treat intellectual history.

For the years immediately preceding the period under consideration
we have Howard Mumford Jones, *The Bright Medusa* (1952) and Henry
F. May, *The End of American Innocence: A Study of the First Years
of Our Own Time, 1912–1917* (1959).

Among the many specialized studies or monographs concerning American thought in the years 1917 to 1930, the following proved especially
valuable: Norman F. Furniss, *The Fundamentalist Controversy, 1918–
1931* (1954); Charles Merz, *The Dry Decade* (1931); James Timber-
lake, *Prohibition and the Progressive Movement* (1963); John Higham,
Strangers in the Land: Patterns of American Nativism, 1860–1925
(1955); Robert K. Murray, *Red Scare: A Study in National Hysteria,
1919–1920* (1955); Allen Guttman, *The Conservative Tradition in America* (1967); John W. Ward, "The Meaning of Lindbergh's Flight,"
American Quarterly, 10 (1958), 3–16; David M. Chalmers, *Hooded
Americanism: The First Century of the Ku Klux Klan* (1965); Charles C.
Alexander, *The Ku Klux Klan in the Southwest* (1965); John Moffatt
Mecklin, *The Ku Klux Klan: A Study of the American Mind* (1924);
Roderick Nash, *Wilderness and the American Mind* (1967); Milton W.
Brown, *American Painting from the Armory Show to the Depression*
(1955); Caroline Ware, *Greenwich Village, 1920–1930* (1935); Fred-
erick J. Hoffman, *Freudianism and the Literary Mind* (1945); Oliver O.
Larkin, *Art and Life in America*, rev. ed. (1960); John Killinger, *Hemingway and the Dead Gods: A Study in Existentialism* (1960); Gilbert
Seldes, *The Seven Lively Arts*, rev. ed. (1957); Lewis Jacobs, *The Rise
of the American Film* (1939); Wayne Andrews, *Architecture, Ambition,
and Americans* (1964); David Felix, *Protest: Sacco-Vanzetti and the Intellectuals* (1965); John R. Tunis, *The American Way in Sport* (1958)·

Rex Lardner, *Ten Heroes of the Twenties* (1966); Gilbert Chase, *America's Music* (1955); William Preston, Jr., *Aliens and Dissenters: Federal Suppression of Radicals, 1903–1933* (1963); Arthur S. Link, "What Happened to the Progressive Movement in the 1920's," *American Historical Review*, 44 (July, 1959), 833–885; Clarke A. Chambers, *Seedtime of Reform: American Social Service and Social Action, 1918–1933* (1963); Yvor Winters, *Primitivism and Decadence: A Study of American Experimental Poetry* (1937).

Individual minds are the basic units in intellectual history. The student of the 1920s is fortunate in having available the following biographies: John Malcolm Brinnin, *The Third Rose: Gertrude Stein and Her World* (1959); Sherman Paul, *Randolph Bourne* (1965); John A. Moreau, *Randolph Bourne: Legend and Reality* (1966); William Manchester, *Disturber of the Peace: The Life of H. L. Mencken* (1951); Charles Angoff, *H. L. Mencken* (1956); Arthur Mizener, *The Far Side of Paradise: A Biography of F. Scott Fitzgerald* (1951); Andrew Turnbull, *Scott Fitzgerald* (1962); Keith Sward, *The Legend of Henry Ford* (1949); Carlos Baker, *Ernest Hemingway: A Life Story* (1969); Oscar Handlin, *Al Smith and His America* (1958); Lawrence W. Levine, *Defender of the Faith, William Jennings Bryan: The Last Decade, 1915–1925* (1965); Mark Schorer, *Sinclair Lewis* (1961); Nancy Barr Mavity, *Sister Aimee* (1931) on Aimee Semple McPherson; William G. McLoughlin, *Billy Sunday Was His Real Name* (1955); Walter S. Ross, *The Last Hero: Charles A. Lindbergh* (1968); Stanley Coben, *A. Mitchell Palmer* (1963); John Gassner, *Eugene O'Neill* (1965); John Tebbel, *George Horace Lorimer and the Saturday Evening Post* (1948); D. Joy Humes, *O. G. Villard: Liberal of the Twenties* (1960); Robert C. Bannister, *Ray Stannard Baker: The Mind and Thought of a Progressive* (1966); William G. McLoughlin, "Aimee Semple McPherson," *Journal of Popular Culture*, 1 (Winter, 1967), 193–217; Edward G. Lueders, *Carl Van Vechten and the Twenties* (1955); Robert Sklar, *F. Scott Fitzgerald, the Last Laocoön* (1967); Brom Weber, *Hart Crane* (1948); R. W. B. Lewis, *The Poetry of Hart Crane* (1967); L. C. Powell, *Robinson Jeffers, The Man and His Work* (1934); Frederick Manchester and Odell Shepard, *Irving Babbitt* (1941); Jacob Zeitlin and Homer Woodbridge, *Life and Letters of Stuart P. Sherman* (1929); E. K. Brown and Leon Edel, *Willa Cather* (1953); Robert Shafer, *Paul Elmer More and American Criticism* (1935); K. W. Detzer, *Carl Sandburg: A Study in Personality* (1941).

Unpublished doctoral dissertations on American thought in the period 1917 to 1930 are numerous and, in some cases, rewarding. Among the best are: Chadwick Hansen, "The Age of Jazz: A Study of Jazz in Its Cultural Context" (University of Minnesota, 1956); Benjamin M. Jeffery, "The *Saturday Evening Post* Short Story in the 1920s" (University of

Texas, 1966); Kenneth K. Bailey, "The Anti-Evolution Crusade of the 1920s" (Vanderbilt University, 1953); Arthur C. Ketels, "The American Drama of the Twenties: A Critical Revaluation" (Northwestern University, 1960); Clair E. Nelsen, "The Image of Herbert Hoover as Reflected in the American Press" (Stanford University, 1956); Forrest W. Frease, "As I Remember: Aspects of American Life Between the First World War and the Second World War as Recalled in Autobiographies" (University of Pennsylvania, 1952); Lucille T. Birnbaum, "Behaviorism: John B. Watson and American Social Thought, 1913–1933" (University of California, Berkeley, 1964); Fred Ragan, "*The New Republic:* Red Hysteria and Civil Liberties" (University of Georgia, 1965); Warren I. Susman, "Pilgrimage to Paris: The Backgrounds of American Expatriation, 1920–1934" (University of Wisconsin, 1957); George S. May, "Ultra-Conservative Thought in the United States in the 1920s and 1930s" (University of Michigan, 1954); Peter J. Schmitt, "The Virgin Land in the Twentieth Century: The Concept of Nature in an Urban Society, 1900–1925" (University of Minnesota, 1967); Robert G. Comegys, "The Agrarian and Rural Traditions as Reflected in National Periodical Literature, 1919–1929" (Stanford University, 1958); Bartlett C. Jones, "The Debate over National Prohibition, 1920–1933" (Emory University, 1961); Don S. Kirschner, "Conflict in the Corn Belt: Rural Reactions to Urbanization in the United States, 1919–1929" (State University of Iowa, 1961); Ronald E. Mickel, "Patterns of Agrarian Self-Consciousness in the 1920s" (Wayne State University, 1961); Joseph E. Clark, "America's Critique of the Democratic Idea" (Stanford University, 1958); Claire Sacks, "The *Seven Arts* Critics: A Study of Cultural Nationalism in America, 1910–1930" (University of Wisconsin, 1955); George Douglas Murphy, "The New Biographers of the 1920s and Their Revaluation of the American Tradition" (University of Pennsylvania, 1964).

Linda Gutowski's "George Gershwin's Relationship to the Search for an American Culture during the 1920s" (University of Maryland, 1967) is a master's thesis of exceptional value.

Index

ELEPHANT PAPERBACKS

American History and American Studies
Stephen Vincent Benét, *John Brown's Body*, EL10
Henry W. Berger, ed., *A William Appleman Williams Reader*, EL126
Andrew Bergman, *We're in the Money*, EL124
Paul Boyer, ed., *Reagan as President*, EL117
Robert V. Bruce, *1877: Year of Violence*, EL102
Philip Callow, *From Noon to Starry Night*, EL37
George Dangerfield, *The Era of Good Feelings*, EL110
Clarence Darrow, *Verdicts Out of Court*, EL2
Floyd Dell, *Intellectual Vagabondage*, EL13
Elisha P. Douglass, *Rebels and Democrats*, EL108
Theodore Draper, *The Roots of American Communism*, EL105
Joseph Epstein, *Ambition*, EL7
Lloyd C. Gardner, *Pay Any Price*, EL136
Lloyd C. Gardner, *Spheres of Influence*, EL131
Paul W. Glad, *McKinley, Bryan, and the People*, EL119
Daniel Horowitz, *The Morality of Spending*, EL122
Kenneth T. Jackson, *The Ku Klux Klan in the City, 1915–1930*, EL123
Edward Chase Kirkland, *Dream and Thought in the Business Community, 1860–1900*, EL114
Herbert S Klein, *Slavery in the Americas*, EL103
Aileen S. Kraditor, *Means and Ends in American Abolitionism*, EL111
Leonard W. Levy, *Jefferson and Civil Liberties: The Darker Side*, EL107
Thomas J. McCormick, *China Market*, EL115
Walter Millis, *The Martial Spirit*, EL104
Nicolaus Mills, ed., *Culture in an Age of Money*, EL302
Nicolaus Mills, *Like a Holy Crusade*, EL129
Roderick Nash, *The Nervous Generation*, EL113
William L. O'Neill, ed., *Echoes of Revolt: The Masses, 1911–1917*, EL5
Gilbert Osofsky, *Harlem: The Making of a Ghetto*, EL133
Edward Pessen, *Losing Our Souls*, EL132
Glenn Porter and Harold C. Livesay, *Merchants and Manufacturers*, EL106
John Prados, *Presidents' Secret Wars*, EL134
Edward Reynolds, *Stand the Storm*, EL128
Richard Schickel, *The Disney Version*, EL135
Edward A. Shils, *The Torment of Secrecy*, EL303
Geoffrey S. Smith, *To Save a Nation*, EL125
Bernard Sternsher, ed., *Hitting Home: The Great Depression in Town and Country*, EL109
Athan Theoharis, *From the Secret Files of J. Edgar Hoover*, EL127
Nicholas von Hoffman, *We Are the People Our Parents Warned Us Against*, EL301
Norman Ware, *The Industrial Worker, 1840–1860*, EL116
Tom Wicker, *JFK and LBJ: The Influence of Personality upon Politics*, EL120
Robert H. Wiebe, *Businessmen and Reform*, EL101
T. Harry Williams, *McClellan, Sherman and Grant*, EL121
Miles Wolff, *Lunch at the 5 & 10*, EL118
Randall B. Woods and Howard Jones, *Dawning of the Cold War*, EL130

ELEPHANT PAPERBACKS

Literature and Letters

24000639R00117

Made in the USA
Columbia, SC
16 August 2018